Dad and I

Dad rakes
the lawn.

I rake the lawn, too!

Dad pulls the weeds.

I pull the weeds, too.

Dad washes the car.

I wash the car, too.

Dad takes a nap.

I take a nap, too. Almost!

What Did It Say?

Mark the things that the girl and her dad did in the story.

______ 1. They baked a cake.

______ 2. They raked the leaves.

______ 3. They read a book.

______ 4. They pulled the weeds.

______ 5. They washed the dog.

______ 6. They washed the car.

Draw something the dad did that the little girl did not do.

Skills: Sequencing Events; Predicting Outcomes

Before and After

Cut and paste to show how each thing looked before and after.

Before		After
paste	**The Lawn** We raked the leaves.	*paste*
paste	**The Weeds** We pulled the weeds.	*paste*
paste	**The Car** We washed the car.	*paste*

Skills: Listening for the /p/ Sound

The Sound of p

Color the pictures that start with the sound **p** stands for.

poodle

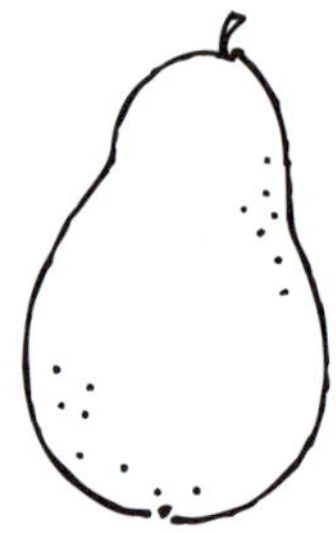

pear

key

ball

penguin

purse

penny

cupcake

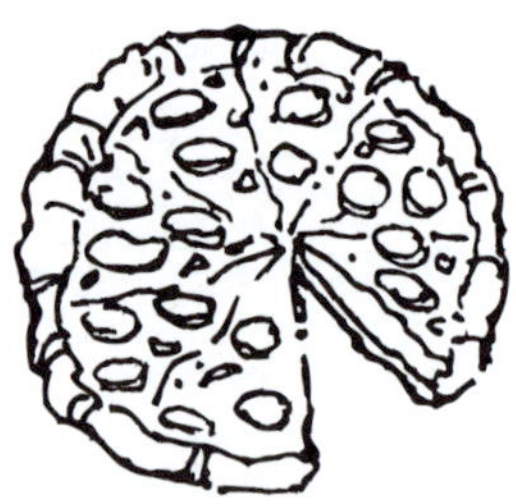

pizza

porcupine

pig

paint

This Is the Way to Wash a Car

Color the pictures. Cut and paste in order the directions for washing a car.

paste

paste

paste

paste

Wash off the dirt.

Dry off the car.

Rinse with clean water.

Get the car wet.

What Do You Hear?

Fill in the circle under the vowel sound you hear.

		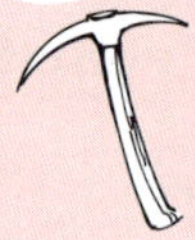		
a	e	i	o	u

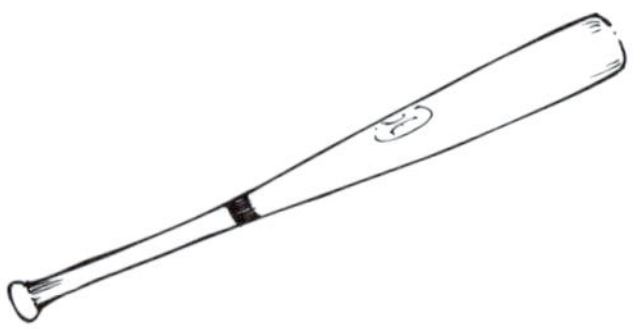 a e i ● ○ ○	 a e o ○ ○ ○	 e i a ○ ○ ○
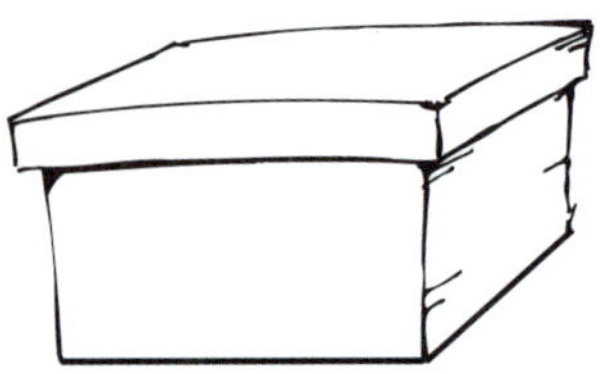 a u o ○ ○ ○	 e o u ○ ○ ○	**6** i e a ○ ○ ○
 o i e ○ ○ ○	 u o i ○ ○ ○	 a u o ○ ○ ○
 e a u ○ ○ ○	 i e a ○ ○ ○	**10** o a e ○ ○ ○

Working with Word Families

ap

n + ap = __ __ __

c + ap = __ __ __

m + ap = __ __ __

scr + ap = __ __ __ __ __

tr + ap = __ __ __ __

str + ap = __ __ __ __ __

Finish the pictures. Then color them.

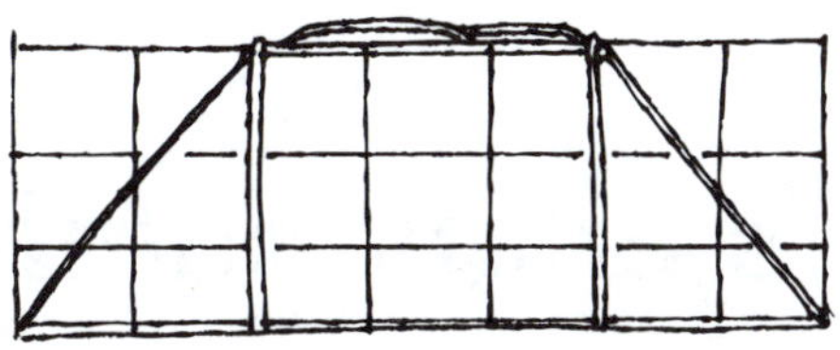

Draw a mouse in the trap.

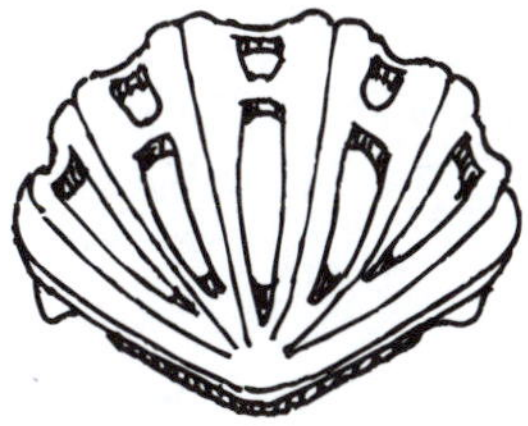

Draw a strap on the helmet.

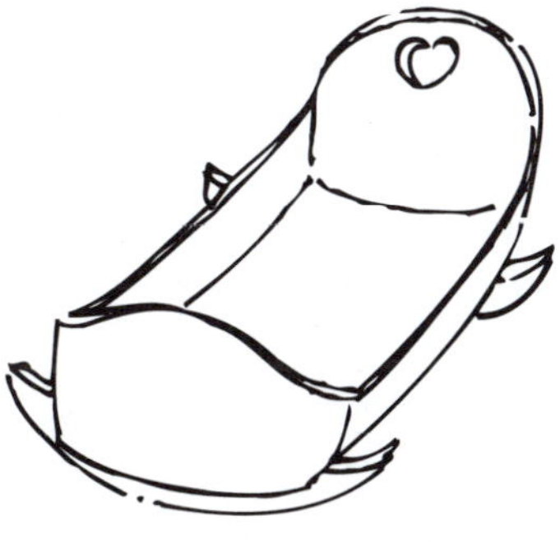

Show the baby taking a nap.

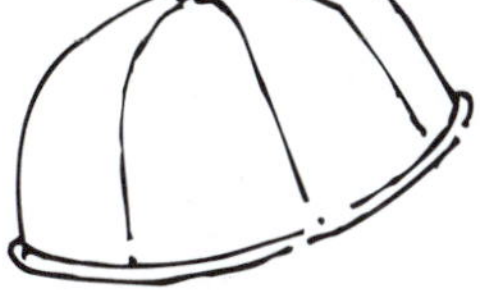

Add a feather and a flower.

My Cocoon

It's cold out there.

It's warm in here.

It's bright out there.

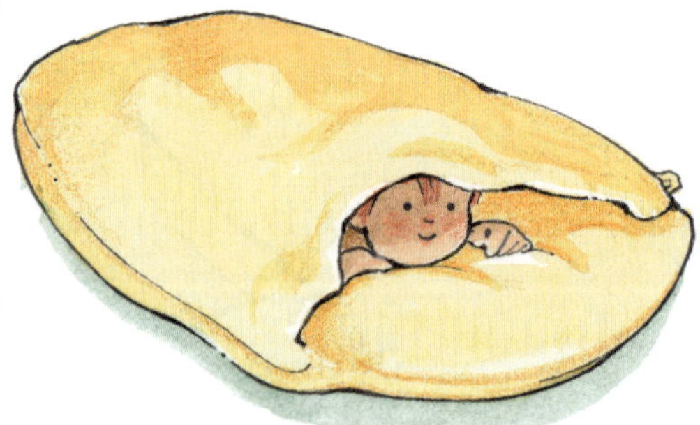

It's dark in here.

It's loud out there.

It's quiet in here.

It's busy out there.

It's still in here.

My sleeping bag is like a cocoon.

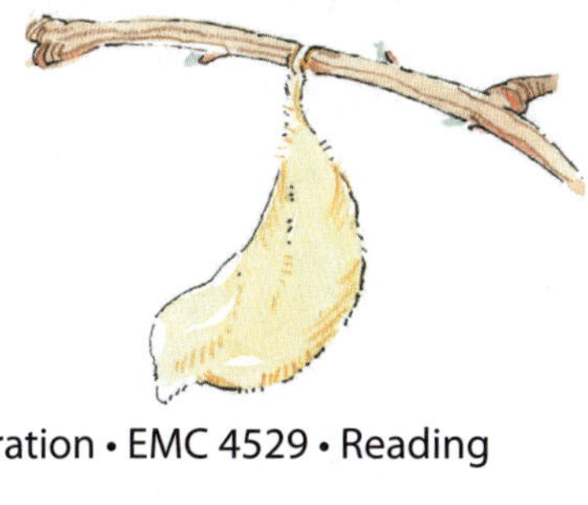

What Did It Say?

Circle the words that tell about the cocoon and the sleeping bag.

cold	quiet	warm	bright
loud	busy	still	dark

Fill in the circle in front of the answer.

1. 

○ It is warm here.
○ It is cold here.

2. 

○ It is dark here.
○ It is bright here.

3. 

○ It is loud here.
○ It is quiet here.

Opposites

Words like **loud** and **quiet** are called **opposites**.
Draw a line to connect the opposites.

My hat is on.

up	clean
high	busy
bright	down
still	slow
fast	dark
dirty	low

My hat is off.

Draw pictures to show the **opposites**.

off	empty
on	full

Real or Make-Believe?

Circle **real** or **make-believe**.

real
make-believe

real
make-believe

real
make-believe

real
make-believe

Draw something about a butterfly that could be real.

Draw something about a butterfly that is make-believe.

Skills: Sequencing Events; Writing a Description

Put It in Order

Color, cut, and paste to put the pictures in order.
Write about each picture.

1.

paste

____

____

____

____

2.

paste

____

____

____

____

3.

paste

____

____

____

____

Working with Word Families

ill

h + ill = __ __ __ __

f + ill = __ __ __ __

ch + ill = __ __ __ __ __

dr + ill = __ __ __ __ __

Use the new words to complete these sentences.

1. Please ___________ my glass with milk.

2. I need a ___________ to fix the door.

3. He lives at the top of the __________.

4. If you go out in the cold you will get

   a ___________.

Skills: Seeing the Whole; Writing a Description

Finish the Picture

Draw the other side of the butterfly. Then color the picture.

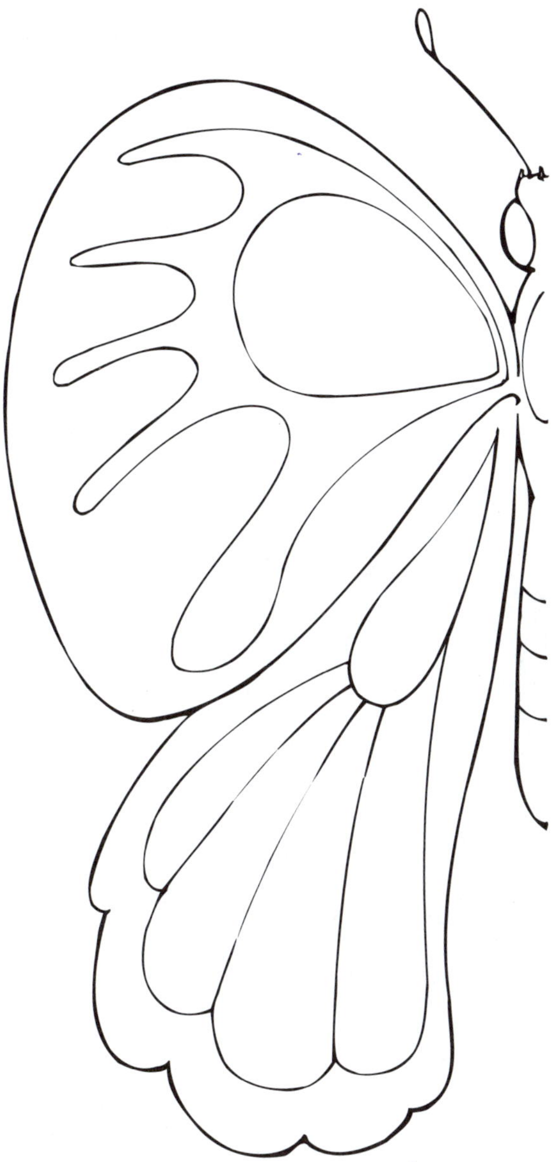

Write about the butterfly.

My butterfly ________________________________

____

____.

Who Can Fix It?

The wheel came
off my car.
Who can fix it?
I know!
Uncle Joe.

The knob came off the door. Who can fix it?
I know! Mr. Snow.

The flower came
off the stem.
Who can fix it?
I know!
Just let the
stem grow.

Skills: Recalling Story Details; Matching Rhyming Words

What Did It Say?

Draw a picture of each thing. Then draw lines to tell who fixed it.

button	Mr. Snow
wheel	Sis
knob	Uncle Joe

Which thing could not be fixed quickly?

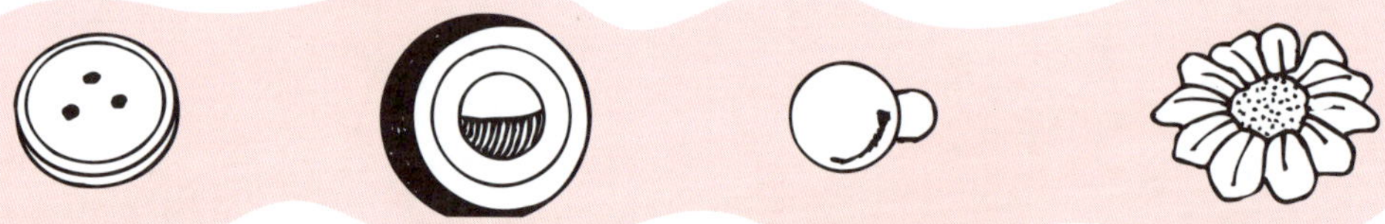

Words That Rhyme

Write the four words in the story that rhyme with **know**.

______________________ ______________________

______________________ ______________________

Skills: Listening for the /b/ Sound

The Same Sound

Color the pictures that begin with the same sound as **button**.

Working with Word Families

ar

j + ar = ___ ___ ___

st + ar = ___ ___ ___ ___

c + ar = ___ ___ ___

b + ar = ___ ___ ___

sc + ar = ___ ___ ___ ___

f + ar = ___ ___ ___

Use the new words to complete these sentences.

I will look at the __________.

I can hang from the high ________.

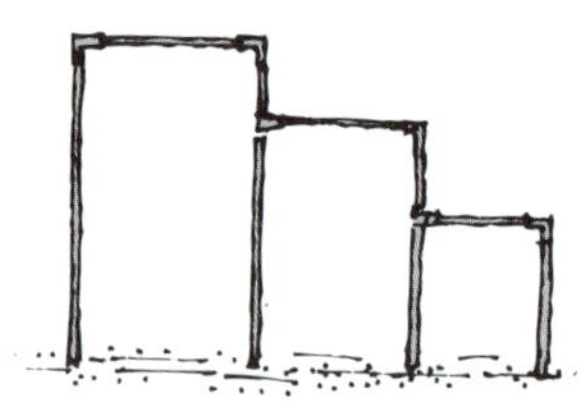

I will put the bug in a _________.

I don't want to have a ________.

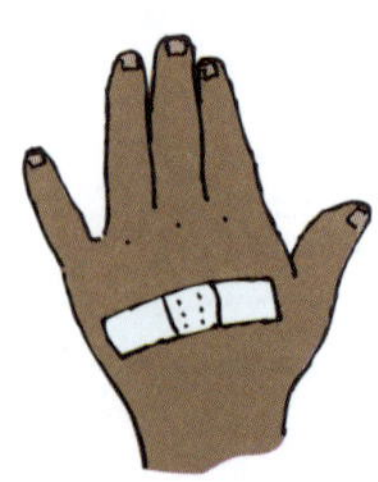

Skills: Comprehending Sentences; Using Prior Knowledge

Will It Work?

Fill in the circle to answer **yes** or **no**.

1. You can fix the pants with a needle and thread.

   ○ yes   ○ no

2. You can fix the toy car with a rubber band.

   ○ yes   ○ no

3. You can fix the doorknob with tape.

   ○ yes   ○ no

4. You can fix the flower with glue.

   ○ yes   ○ no

What would you use to fix a cut on your hand?

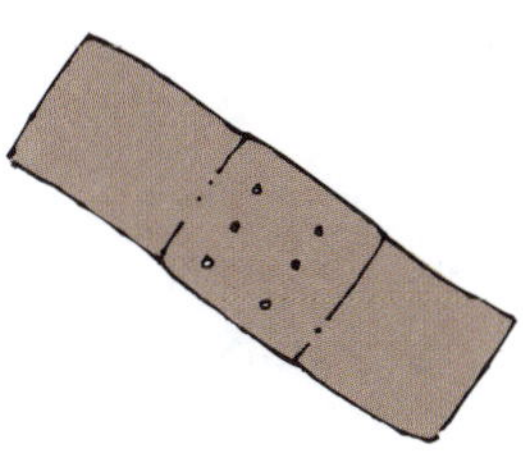

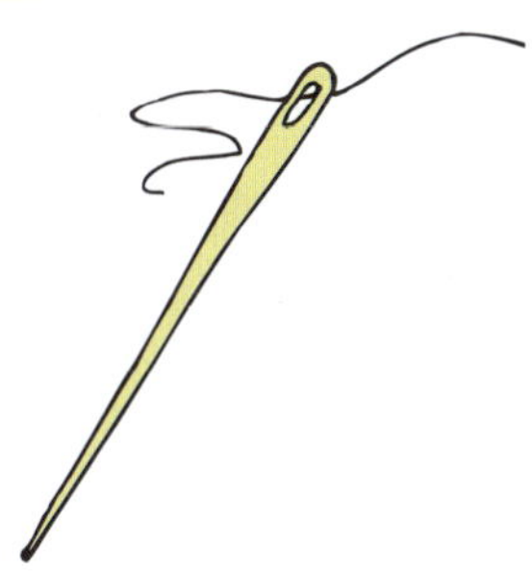

Reading Color Words

Read the words. Color the buttons.

blue

red

orange

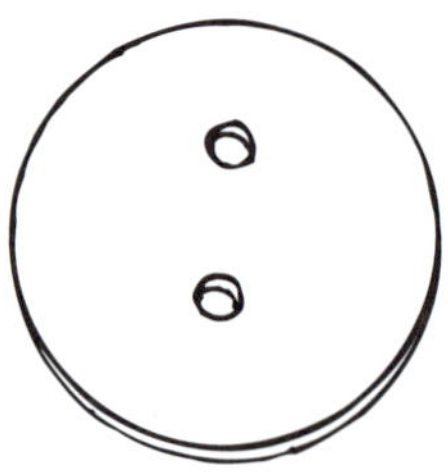

green

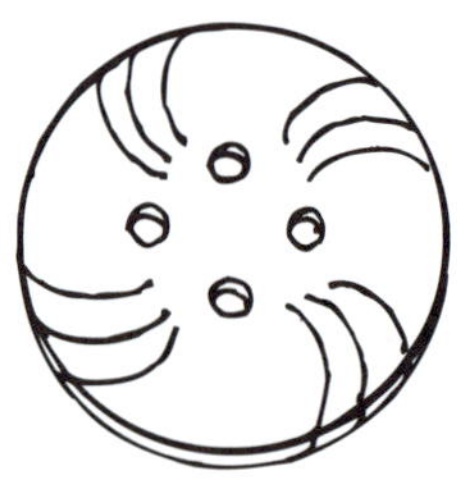

purple

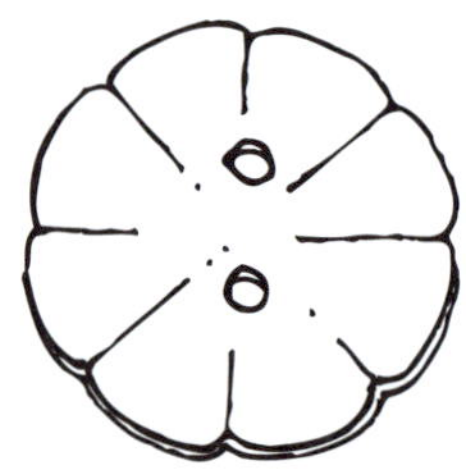

brown

pink

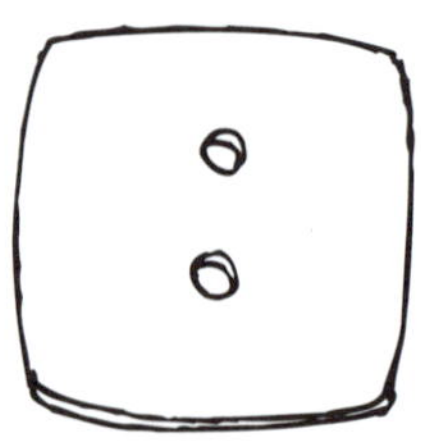

yellow

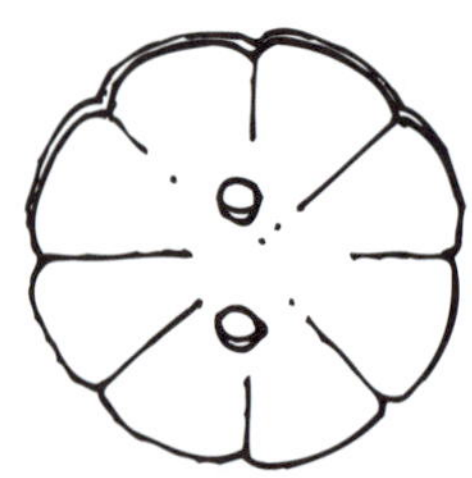

black

Skills: Identifying Long Vowel Sounds

What Do You Hear?

Fill in the circle under the vowel sound you hear.

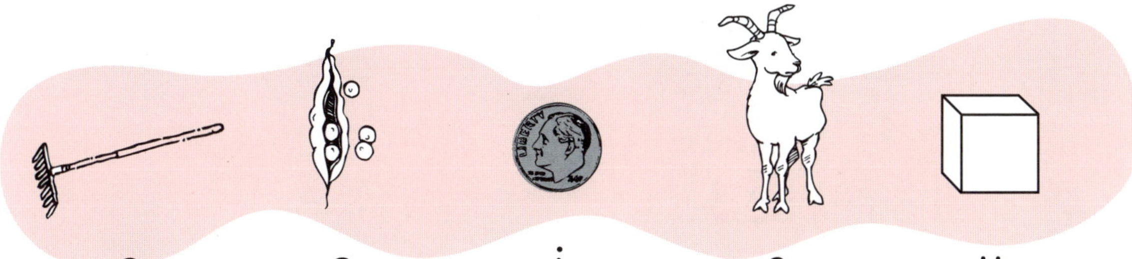

a e i o u

a e i

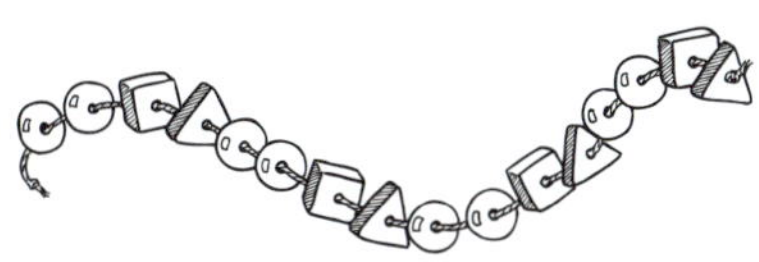

a e o

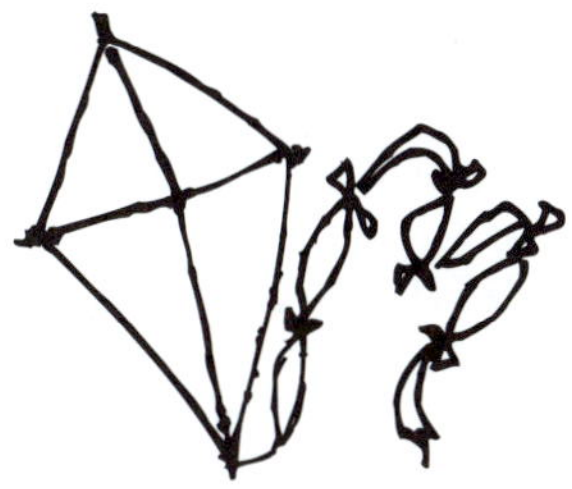

e i a

a u o

e a u

i e o

o i e

a u o

e i o

Giant Tortoise

Step by step—see it go.
Step by step—soooo slow.

Heavy shell on its back.
Heavy shell—like a pack.

Plodding on in the sand.
Plodding on over land.

Step by step—see it go.
Step by step—soooo slow.

After You Read

Practice reading the poem.
Make it sound slow like a tortoise.
Read it to an adult.

What Did It Say?

Fill in the circle for the correct answer.

1. How does the tortoise move?
   - ○ It moves fast.
   - ○ It moves quickly.
   - ○ It moves slowly.

2. What is the tortoise's shell like?
   - ○ It's like a tent.
   - ○ It's like a pack.
   - ○ It's like a suitcase.

3. Where does the tortoise walk?
   - ○ It walks in the woods.
   - ○ It walks in the snow.
   - ○ It walks in the sand.

Draw a picture of a giant tortoise here.

Working with Word Families

ell

b + ell = __ __ __ __

t + ell = __ __ __ __

sh + ell = __ __ __ __ __

w + ell = __ __ __ __

sm + ell = __ __ __ __ __

sp + ell = __ __ __ __ __

Write one of the new words in each sentence. Then draw a picture to show what the sentence says.

The snail has a hard ____________.

I can ____________ the pretty rose.

The ____________ rings when school starts.

I threw a penny in the wishing ____________.

Skills: Categorizing; Understanding Opposites (Antonyms)

Heavy or Light?

Color, cut, and paste. Show which things are **heavy** and which things are **light**.

light

heavy

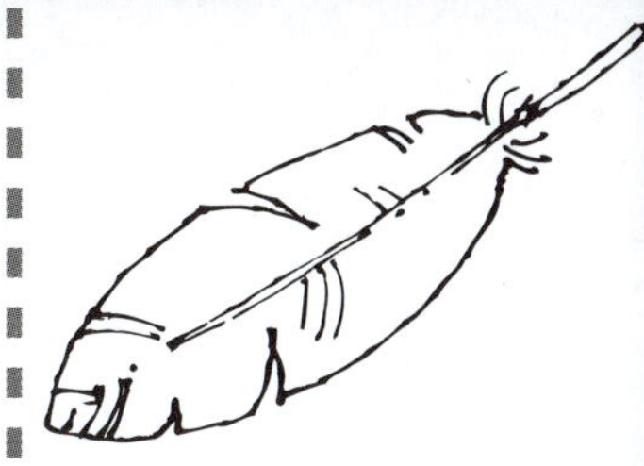

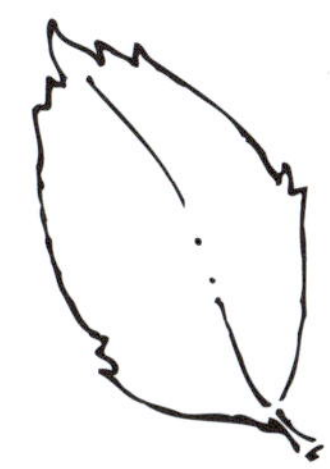

Skills: Following Directions; Writing a Description

Cool, Man, Cool!

The tortoise wants to look cool. Can you color its shell in a special way? Add shoes and a hat.

Tell what the tortoise looks like.

____

____.

In a Shell

Draw another animal that lives in a shell.
Draw the place where it lives, too.

I am a ________________________________.

I live ________________________________

____

____.

Put It in the Pack

I'm going on a camping trip.
I will put the things
I need in my pack.

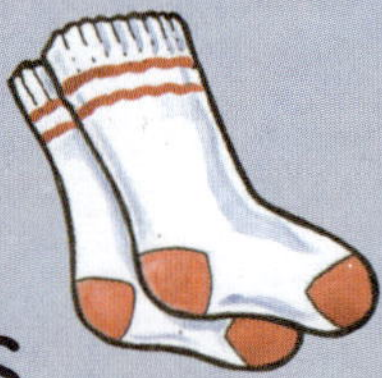

I'll need socks.

I'll need a shirt.

I'll need shorts.

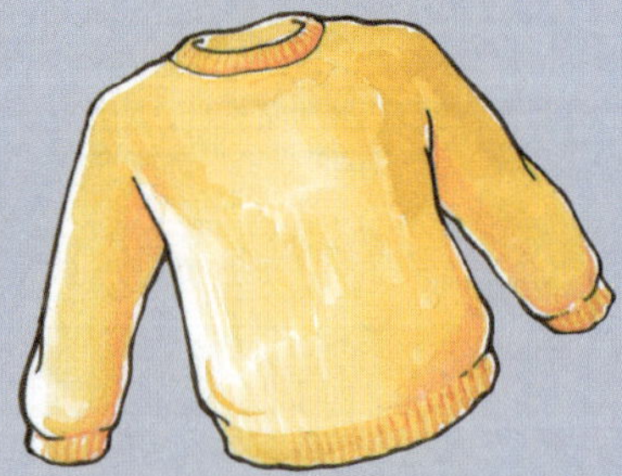

I'll need a sweatshirt.

Put it in the pack.

I'll need a hat.

I'll need food.

I'll need my sleeping bag.

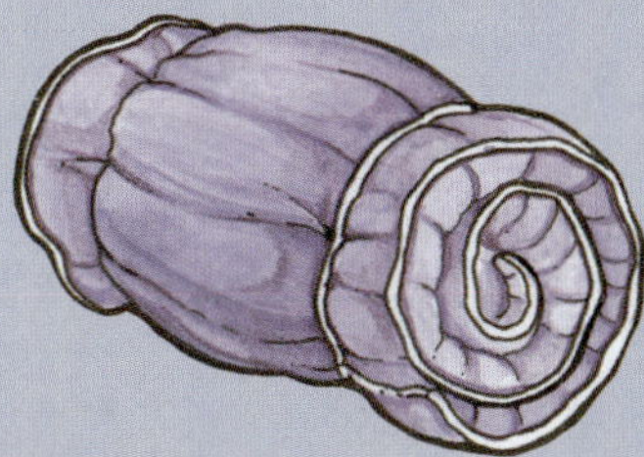

I'll need a flashlight.

I'll need Teddy.

Put me in the pack!

I'll put the pack on my back.

Help! I can't move.

I can't hike to the camp.

I'll take out a few things.

I don't have to have socks.

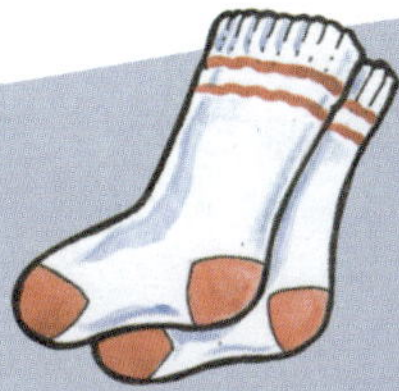

I don't have to have a shirt.

I don't have to have shorts.

I don't have to have a sweatshirt.

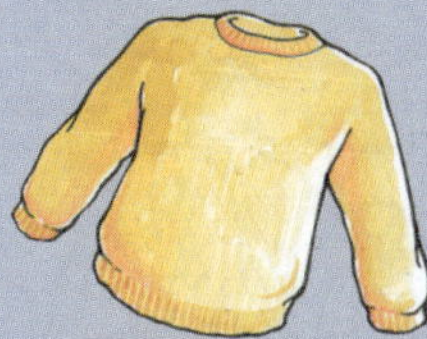

I don't have to have a hat.

I don't have to have food.

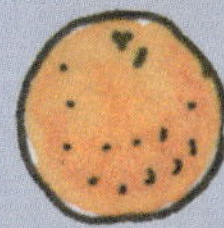

I don't have to have a sleeping bag.

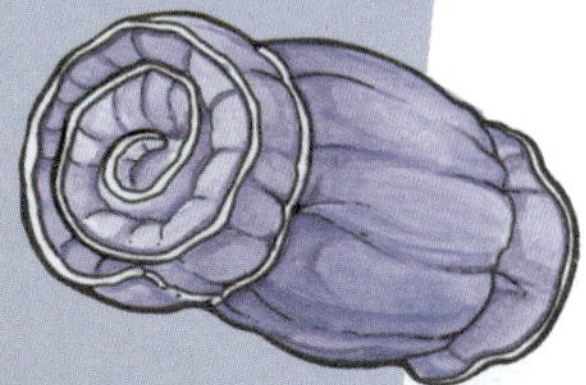

I don't have to have a flashlight.

Teddy and I are ready!

Let's go!

After You Read

Practice reading this page. When you can read it with no mistakes, read it to an adult.

What Did It Say?

Fill in a circle to answer each question.

1. Where is the little girl going?

2. How will the little girl carry her things?

3. What is the little girl's problem?

4. What does the little girl take out that she will need?

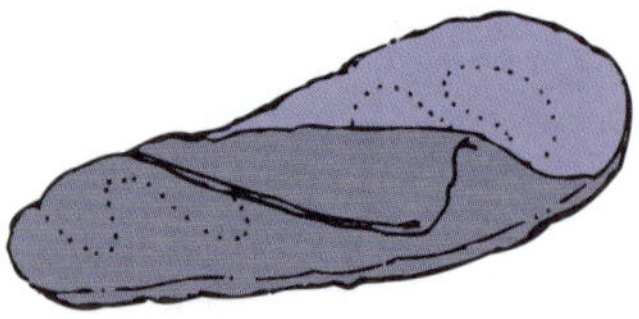  

Working with Word Families

ack

b + ack = ___ ___ ___ ___

p + ack = ___ ___ ___ ___

cr + ack = ___ ___ ___ ___ ___

qu + ack = ___ ___ ___ ___ ___

sn + ack = ___ ___ ___ ___ ___

tr + ack = ___ ___ ___ ___ ___

s + ack = ___ ___ ___ ___

r + ack = ___ ___ ___ ___

Read the sentence in each box. Draw what it tells you to do.

Draw a dish with a crack.	Draw a snack you like to eat.

Skills: Logical Thinking; Categorizing

What Would You Do?

Fill in the circle for the correct answer.

What would you do if your pack was too heavy?

○ Take something out. ○ Put something in.

What would you do if it got dark?

○ Turn off the flashlight. ○ Turn on the flashlight.

What would you do if you got hungry?

○ Eat a snack. ○ Go to bed.

What would you do to stay dry in the rain?

○ Go outside. ○ Go in the tent.

What would you cook on the fire?

○ Hot dogs and marshmallows ○ Jello and ice cream

Take It Camping!

Circle the things you would take camping.

Draw a line under the ones you would need for school.

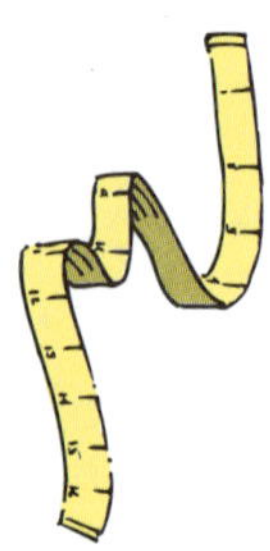

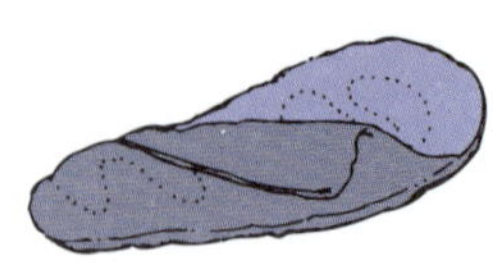

Connect the Dots

Start with 1. Make something you might see on a camping trip.

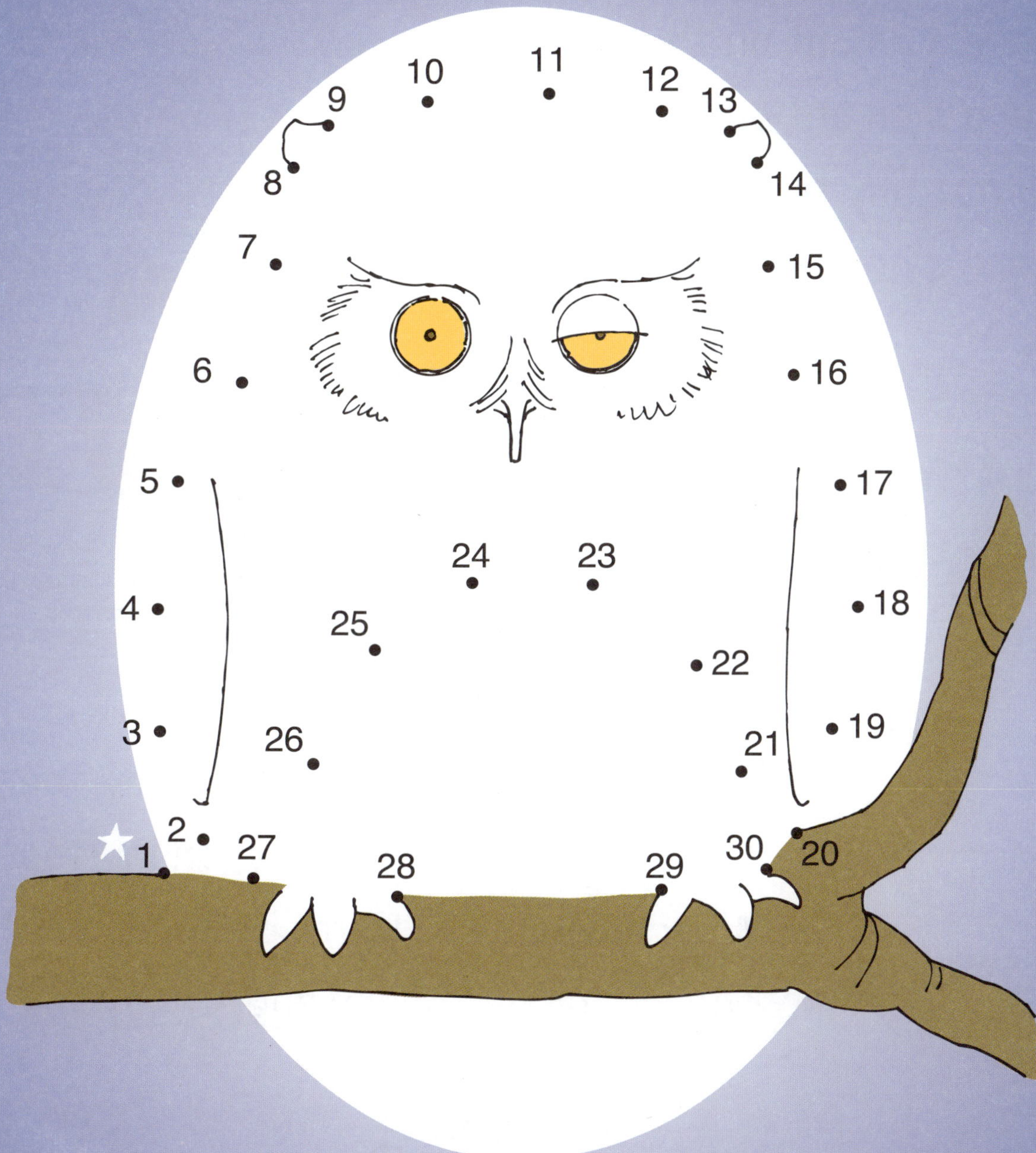

Make a list of animals you might see on a camping trip.

An Ant on the Rug

There's an ant on the rug, on the rug.
There's an ant on the rug, on the rug.
What a tiny bug, little ant on the rug.
There's an ant on the rug, on the rug.

There's an ant on my toe, on my toe.
There's an ant on my toe, on my toe.
Where will it go, that ant on my toe?
There's an ant on my toe, on my toe.

There's an ant on my knee, on my knee.
There's an ant on my knee, on my knee.
It's climbing up on me. Ooooo! An ant on my knee.
There's an ant on my knee, on my knee.

There's an ant on my arm, on my arm.
There's an ant on my arm, on my arm.
It won't do any harm, the ant on my arm.
There's an ant on my arm, on my arm.

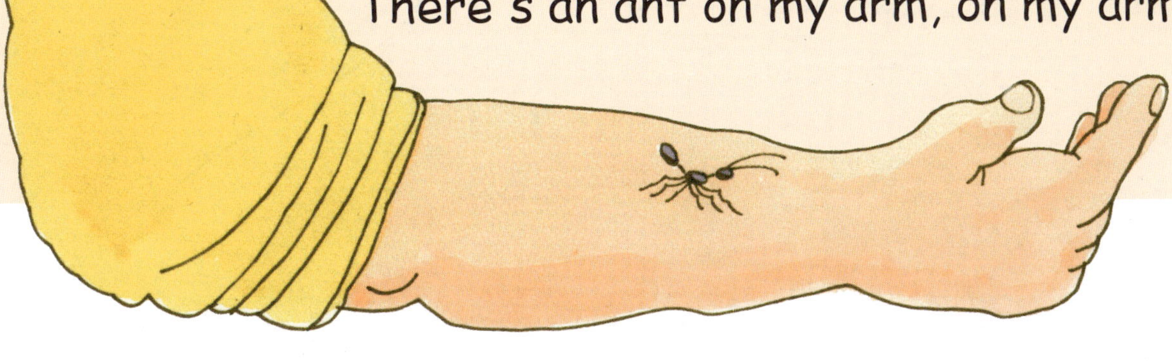

There's an ant on my ear, on my ear.
There's an ant on my ear, on my ear.
I have nothing to fear from the ant on my ear.
There's an ant on my ear, on my ear.

There's an ant on my nose, on my nose.
There's an ant on my nose, on my nose.
What do you suppose? An ant on my nose!
There's an ant on my nose, on my nose.

There's an ant in my hair, in my hair.
There's an ant in my hair, in my hair.
I am very aware there's an ant in my hair.
There's an ant in my hair, in my hair.

There's an ant in a jar, in a jar.
There's an ant in a jar, in a jar.
It traveled near and far,
but now it's in a jar.
There's an ant in a jar, in a jar.

After You Read

Practice your favorite part of the story. When you can read it quickly, read it to an adult.

What Did It Say?

Draw a line to show where the ant was.

First 

Next 

Next 

Next 

Next 

Next 

Next 

At the end 

Do you think the boy was happy to have the ant in the jar?

yes no

Why do you think the way you do?

____

____

Working with Word Families

ug

r + ug = ___ ___ ___

b + ug = ___ ___ ___

d + ug = ___ ___ ___

h + ug = ___ ___ ___

pl + ug = ___ ___ ___ ___

sn + ug = ___ ___ ___ ___

Use the new words to complete these sentences.

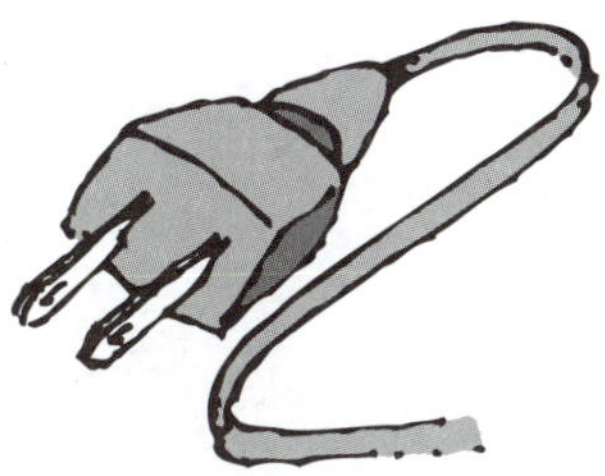

Be careful when you touch the __________.

Look at the hole I __________.

Dad gave me a __________.

He's as __________ as a __________ in a __________.

Same Sound

Color the pictures that have the same **a** sound as  .

flag

pants

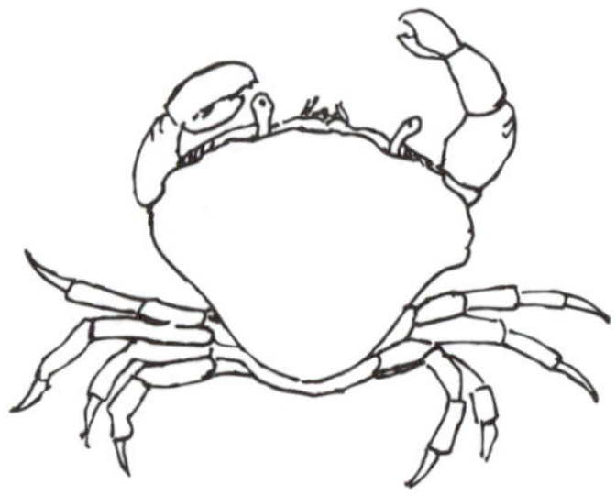

crab

lamb

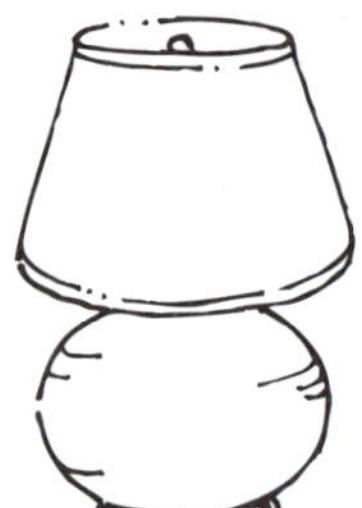

lamp

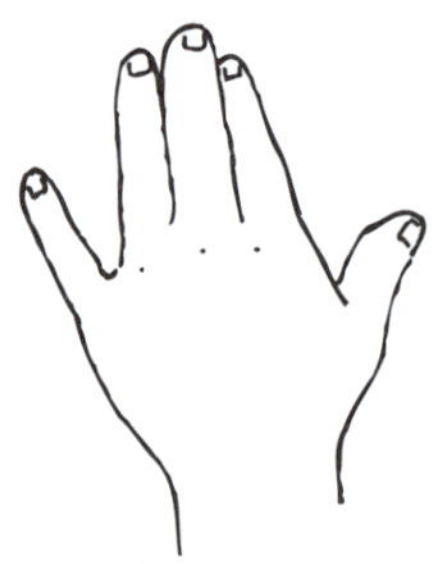

hand

piggy bank

apple

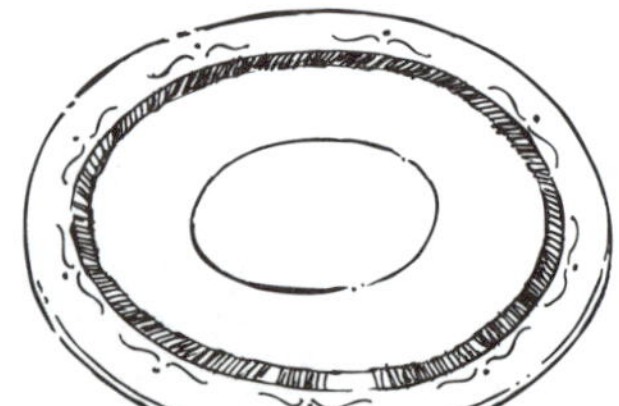

plate

What Does It Mean?

Cut and paste to label the picture.

hair

nose

ear

arm

knee

toe

Skills: Listening for Rhyming Words; Recognizing Words

Rhyme Time

Color the pictures in each row that rhyme.
Write the words under the pictures.

 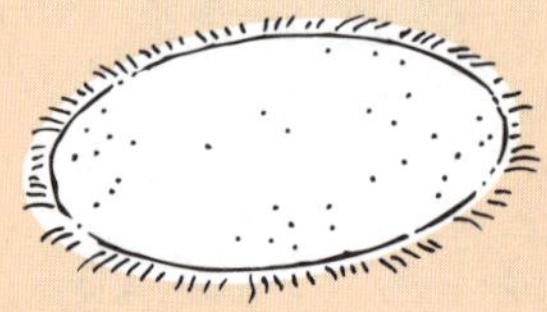 

__________ __________ __________

__________ __________ __________

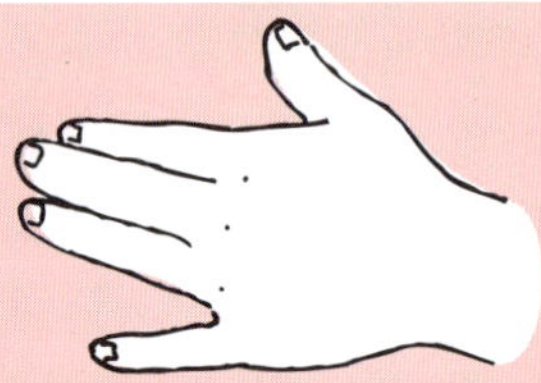 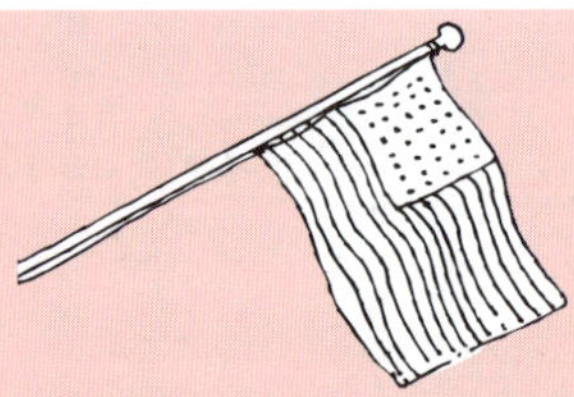 

__________ __________ __________

bell	flag	hen	rug
bug	fan	pen	sand
car	hand	plate	skate

Who Lives in the Barn?

Cut out the flaps on the other side of this page.
Paste them on the story pages to make a flap book.

Who lives in the big red barn?

He's big and brown.
He shakes his head.
He stamps his foot.
He whinnies at me.

paste 1

The horse, of course.

Who lives in the big red barn?

paste 2

Wow, a cow!

She flips her tail.
She wiggles her ears.
She nuzzles her calf.
She moos at me.

Who lives in the big red barn?

He's big and brown.
He shakes his head.
He stamps his foot.
He whinnies at me.

Who lives in the big red barn?

She flips her tail.
She wiggles her ears.
She nuzzles her calf.
She moos at me.

8
9
7
1
2
6
3
5
4

Who lives in the big red barn?

He's big and brown.
He shakes his head.
He stamps his foot.
He whinnies at me.

paste 1

The horse, of course.

Who lives in the big red barn?

paste 2

Wow, a cow!

She flips her tail.
She wiggles her ears.
She nuzzles her calf.
She moos at me.

Who lives in the big red barn?

She wears her winter coat.
She has a little bell.
She wakes her lamb.
She baas at me.

paste 3

My sheep's asleep.

Who lives in the big red barn?

paste 4

Let's follow the swallow.

It flies from the roof.
It builds a small nest.
It sits on its eggs.
It peeps at me.

Who lives in the big red barn?

He stands by the door.
He runs to me.
He licks my hand.
He barks at me.

paste 5

Not a frog! It's my dog.

Who lives in the big red barn?

She laps the milk.
She licks her paws.
She feeds her kittens.
She purrs at me.

paste 6

*Mother cat!
Think of that.*

Who lives in the big red barn?

It runs so fast.
It hides so well.
It nibbles food.
It squeaks at me.

paste 7

The barn is a house for the mouse.

Who lives in the big red barn?

paste 8

A horse,
A cow,
A sheep,
A swallow,
A dog,
A cat,
And a mouse.
That's who!

paste 9

What Did It Say?

Fill in the circle under the correct answer.

1. Who builds a small nest?

sheep	swallow	cat	mouse
○	○	○	○

2. Who nibbles food?

sheep	swallow	cat	mouse
○	○	○	○

3. Who has a lamb?

sheep	swallow	cat	mouse
○	○	○	○

4. Who flips her tail?

horse	cow	dog	cat
○	○	○	○

5. Who licks a paw?

horse	cow	dog	cat
○	○	○	○

6. Who barks?

horse	cow	dog	cat
○	○	○	○

7. Who stamps a foot?

horse	cow	dog	cat
○	○	○	○

Working with Word Families

ake

c + ake = __ __ __ __

sn + ake = __ __ __ __ __

r + ake = __ __ __ __

sh + ake = __ __ __ __ __

fl + ake = __ __ __ __ __

br + ake = __ __ __ __ __

Write the correct **-ake** word to finish each sentence.
Draw a picture to show what the sentence says.

I ________ up the leaves.

A __________ of snow is on my nose.

Which Came First?

Cut and paste to put the animals in order.
Use the rhyme to help.

Who lives in the barn?

The *paste*, of course.

Wow, a *paste*!

My *paste* is asleep.

Let's follow the *paste*.

Not a frog! It's my *paste*.

Think of that, Mother *paste*!

The barn is a house for the *paste*.

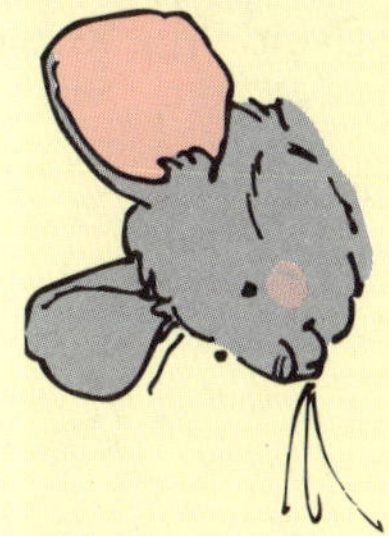

mouse

sheep

dog

swallow

cat

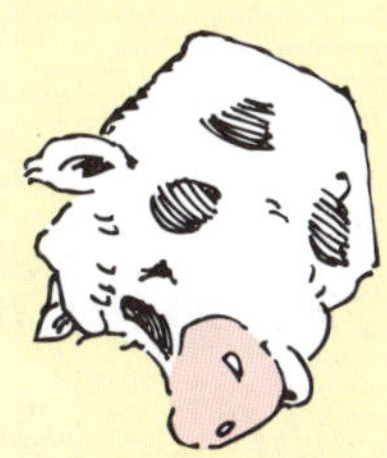

cow

horse

What Does It Say?

Match the noise word to the animal that makes that noise.

baa	
whinny	
purr	
squeak	
chirp	
moo	
woof	

Draw another animal here.
What noise does it make?
It says

______________________.

Skills: Categorizing; Using Prior Knowledge

Think About It

Which animals live mainly on a farm?
Which animals live mainly in the jungle?
Write the names of the animals in the correct list.

goat

lion

elephant

chicken

horse

zebra

cow

monkey

On a farm	In the jungle

The Big Red Barn

Read the color words. Then color the picture.

The Fix-It Man

The fix-it man came to my house.
He fixed the stove.

The fix-it man came to my house.
He fixed the sink.

The fix-it man came to my house.
He fixed the door.

The fix-it man came to my house
He fixed the window.

The fix-it man came to my house.
We had cookies and milk.

What Did It Say?

Fill in the circle by the correct answer.

1. Who did the boy call for help?
   ○ Mother ○ a friend ○ Mr. Fix-It

2. What was wrong with the window?
   ○ It was stuck. ○ It broke. ○ It needed washing.

3. Was Mr. Fix-It a good fixer?
   ○ No, he had to keep coming back.
   ○ Yes, he won a prize.
   ○ Yes, he fixed everything.

4. Why do you think the boy called Mr. Fix-It the last time?
   ○ There were too many cookies in the jar.
   ○ The milk was going to spoil.
   ○ Mr. Fix-It should have a treat.

Write an answer.
Who fixes things at your house?

____

____

____

Skills: Sequencing Events

Put It in Order

Mr. Fix-It will fix the wagon. Color the pictures. Cut and paste to put them in the correct order.

1

paste

2

paste

3

paste

4

paste

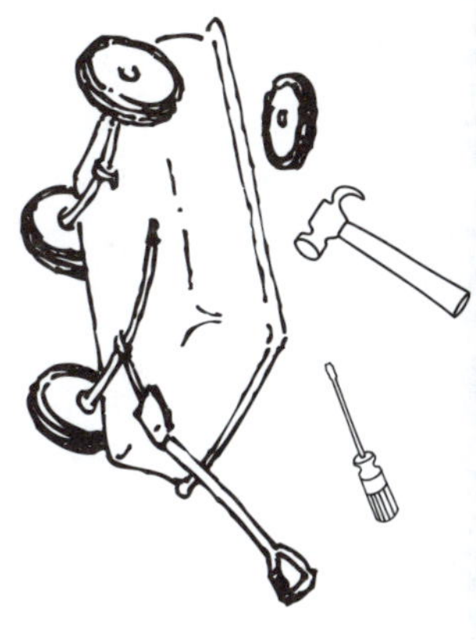

Can It Be Fixed?

Some things cannot be put back together. Write It can be fixed or It can't by each of the pictures below. Use your best handwriting.

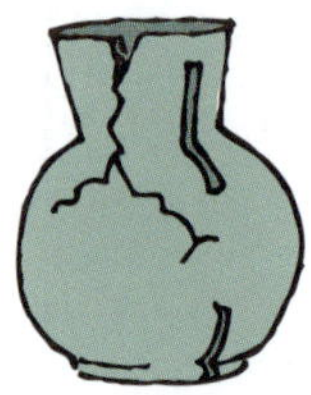

It can't

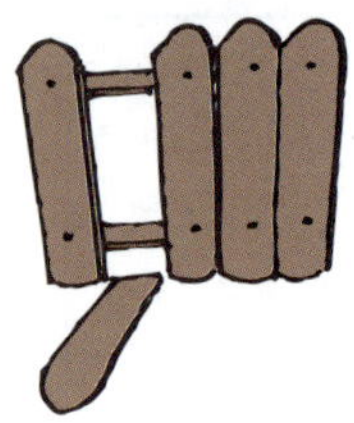

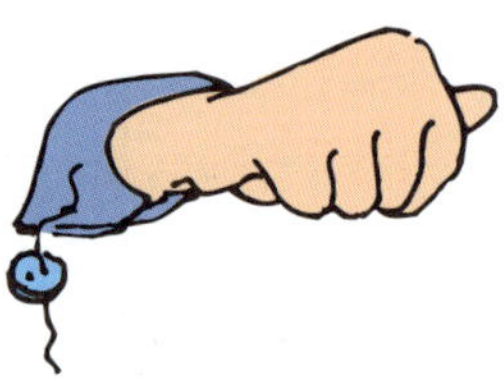

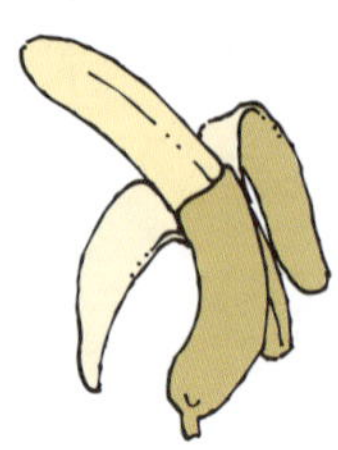

Skills: Blending Words in the –*ink* Family; Following Directions

Working with Word Families

ink

p + ink = ___ ___ ___ ___

s + ink = ___ ___ ___ ___

bl + ink = ___ ___ ___ ___ ___

dr + ink = ___ ___ ___ ___ ___

shr + ink = ___ ___ ___ ___ ___ ___

th + ink = ___ ___ ___ ___ ___

Draw a toy boat in a sink.	Draw a muddy pig that's pink.

More Than One

Add **s** to each word to mean **more than one**.
Then draw what the words say.

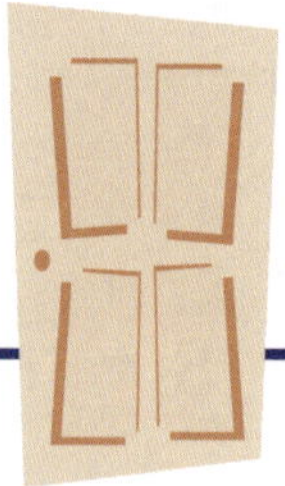

one door

two ____________

one house

three ____________

one bird

four ____________

one flower

five ____________

Rhyme Time

Color the pictures. Circle the words that rhyme.

house

mouse

cat

window

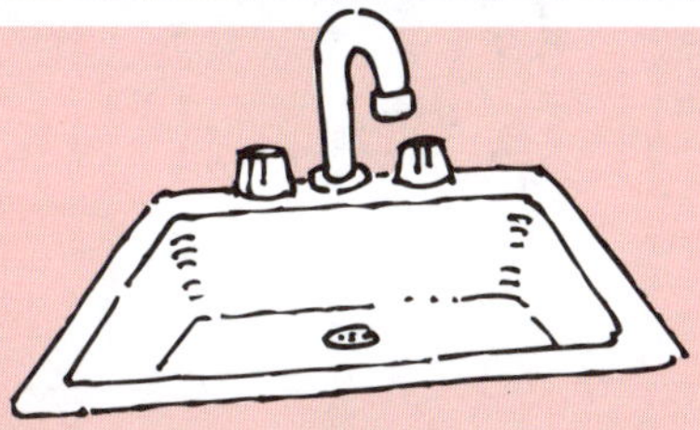

sink

ink

door

bear

chair

dish

milk

fish

cake

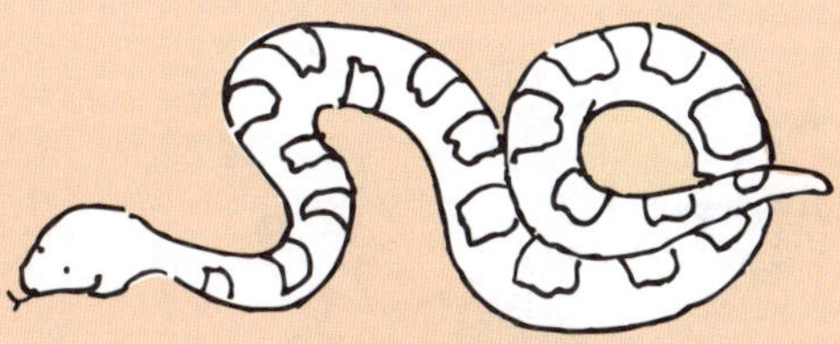

snake

hat

What a

M

Monday
I have muffins.
Munch! Munch!

T

Tuesday
I have tuna.
Tasty!

W

Wednesday
I have waffles.
Wow!

Th

Thursday
I have Thanksgiving turkey.
Thanks!

Week!

Friday
I have fries.
Free fries!

Saturday
I have sodas.
Sip it!

Sunday
I have soup.
See it simmer.

Ummmm—What can I eat next week?

What Did I Have?

Fill in the circle under the correct answer.

1. What did I have on Tuesday?

 turkey ○
 tuna ○
 soup ○

2. What did I have on Friday?

 waffles ○
 muffins ○

fries ○

3. What did I have on Sunday?

 soup ○
 soda ○
 turkey ○

4. What did I have on Monday?

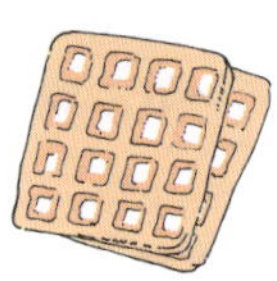 waffles ○

fries ○
 muffins ○

5. What did I have on Saturday?

 soup ○
 soda ○
 tuna ○

My Favorite Foods

Rewrite the story. Draw or write what you would like to eat each day. Then read the story using your foods.

Monday
I have

Tuesday
I have

Wednesday
I have

Thursday
I have

Friday
I have

Saturday
I have

Sunday
I have

Working with Word Families

unch

l + unch = __ __ __ __ __

m + unch = __ __ __ __ __

b + unch = __ __ __ __ __

p + unch = __ __ __ __ __

cr + unch = __ __ __ __ __ __

Circle each word from the **-unch** family in the story below. Draw pictures to show the animals eating.

See the goats?
They like to eat.
Munch, munch,
Hay for lunch.

See the squirrels?
They like to eat.
Munch, munch,
Hear the crunch.

See the monkeys?
They like to eat.
Munch, munch,
What a bunch!

Skills: Categorizing; Using Real-Life Experiences

Noisy Foods

Some foods are noisy. Color the things that make crunchy noises when you eat them. Write **munch** under the ones you like to eat.

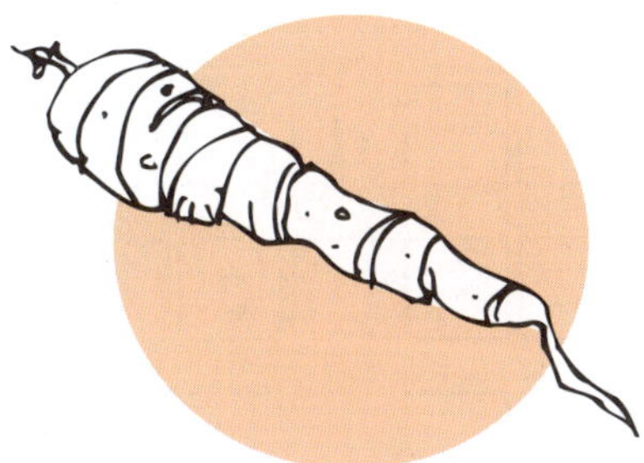

How Does It Taste?

Write one letter of the food name in each box. When all the boxes have been filled in, read the secret message in the pink boxes.

Foods

milk	apple	custard
fruit	cookie	bread
eggs	chocolate	pudding

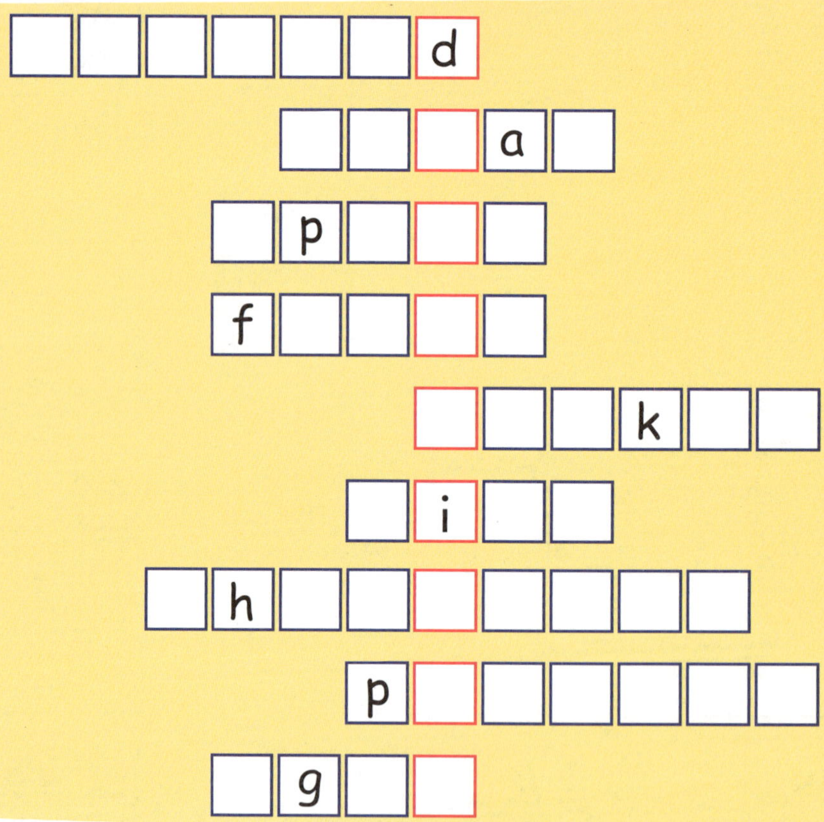

Write the secret message here: ______________________

Food Word Search

See how many of the foods in the Word Box you can find.

Word Box

❑ apple	❑ banana	❑ spaghetti
❑ cookie	❑ pizza	❑ cheese
❑ grapes	❑ pancake	☑ hamburger
❑ orange	❑ carrot	❑ tuna
❑ potatoes	❑ eggs	❑ corn

h	a	m	b	u	r	g	e	r	t	w
a	p	p	l	e	c	a	r	p	u	p
n	c	g	r	a	p	e	s	i	n	o
c	a	t	r	u	c	k	s	z	a	t
o	r	c	h	e	e	s	e	z	x	a
o	r	j	c	o	r	n	z	a	m	t
k	o	p	a	n	c	a	k	e	y	o
i	t	r	a	b	b	i	t	u	p	e
e	r	b	a	n	a	n	a	x	t	s
p	s	p	a	g	h	e	t	t	i	z
o	r	a	n	g	e	w	e	g	g	s

Molly and Max

They played together all week.

Monday they played hide and seek.

Molly hid under the blanket.

Max hid behind the plant.

Tuesday they dug holes in the yard.
Molly buried a bone.
Max picked some flowers.

Wednesday they went for a walk.
Molly walked and sniffed.
Max walked round and round.

Thursday they learned to open doors.
Molly went in and out.
Max found the trash.

Friday they practiced jumping.
Molly jumped high.
Max jumped too high.

Saturday they chased balls.
Molly brought the balls back.
Max found a bigger ball.

Sunday is a day for rest.
Molly will rest.
Will Max rest, too?

What Did It Say?

Fill in the circles to answer the questions.

1. Which dog hid under the blanket? ○ Max ○ Molly
2. Which dog found the trash? ○ Max ○ Molly
3. Which dog brought the balls back? ○ Max ○ Molly
4. Which dog buried a bone? ○ Max ○ Molly
5. Which dog popped a balloon? ○ Max ○ Molly
6. Which dog picked some flowers? ○ Max ○ Molly
7. Which dog do you think will try to open the gifts? ○ Max ○ Molly
8. Which dog is easier to care for? ○ Max ○ Molly

Skills: Sequencing Events

Max Learns the Hard Way

Color, cut, and paste. Put the pictures in order to tell Max's story.

1

paste

2

paste

3

paste

4

paste

Trouble!

It's easy for Max to get in trouble. Put a check by the things that would mean **trouble**.

- ☐ Max chewed the shoe.
- ☐ Max drank his water.
- ☐ Max jumped over the gate.
- ☐ Max chewed on the bone.
- ☐ Max knocked over the lamp.
- ☐ Max picked some flowers.
- ☐ Max took a nap.
- ☐ Max opened the gifts.

Think about what Max might do next.
Write it here.

____

Will it mean trouble for Max? yes no

Working with Word Families

one

b + one = __ __ __ __

c + one = __ __ __ __

ph + one = __ __ __ __ __

st + one = __ __ __ __ __

thr + one = __ __ __ __ __ __

z + one = __ __ __ __

Write the words to label the pictures.

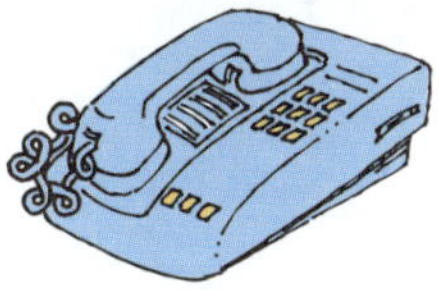

__ __ __ __ __

__ __ __ __

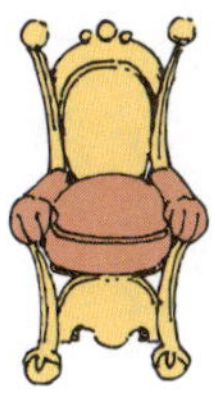

__ __ __ __ __ __

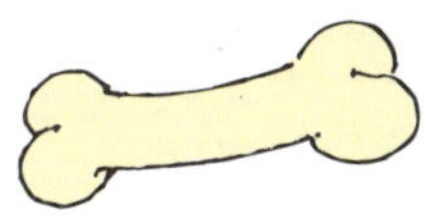

__ __ __ __

__ __ __ __ __

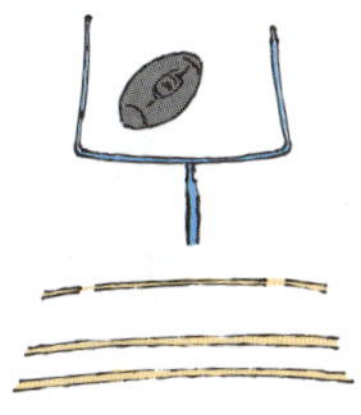

end __ __ __ __

What's at the End?

Write the letter that stands for the sound you hear at the end of each word.

do__

ba__

cu__

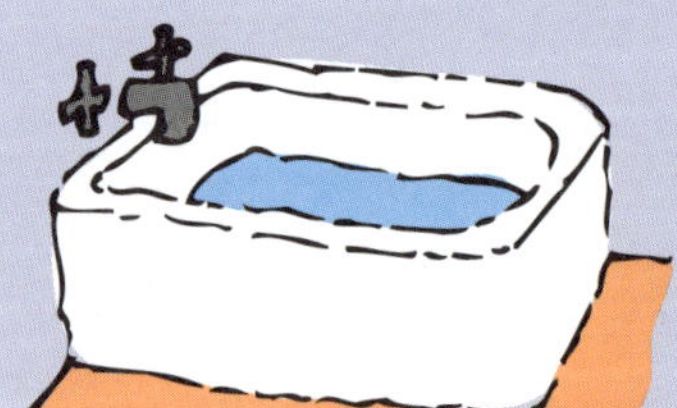
tu__

ca__

doo__

boo__

ja__

ma__

bo__

Skills: Following Directions; Seeing the Whole; Writing a Comparison

Draw a Pup

Follow the steps to draw a puppy.

How is the pup like Max?

____

How is the pup different from Max?

____

New Friends

Cookie lived with Amy. She had a dish for water. She had a dish for food. She had a purple mouse with a long tail. She had all that she needed. Cookie loved her home.

One day Amy came home. She had a surprise for Cookie. It was not a new mouse. It was not a new dish. It was a new friend. It was a little gray kitten.

Cookie didn't need a new friend. Cookie ran from Amy. She hid behind the chair.

The new kitten sniffed Cookie's dish. Cookie hissed at the kitten.

The new kitten tasted Cookie's water. Cookie swatted at the kitten.

The new kitten batted Cookie's mouse. Cookie chased the kitten away.

The new kitten cried. It was afraid. Cookie looked at the kitten. It was shaking.

Cookie touched the kitten with her paw. The kitten was soft. Cookie licked the kitten's ear. She licked the kitten's face. The little kitten began to purr.

Cookie didn't need a friend. But the new kitten did. Maybe Cookie could be the new kitten's friend.

Cookie sat on Amy's lap. The little kitten sat next to Cookie. Cookie purred. The little kitten purred.

Cookie played with her mouse. The little kitten played, too.

Cookie curled up for a nap. The little kitten slept. The little kitten had a new friend. Cookie had a new friend, too.

What Did It Say?

Answer each question.
Fill in the circle to mark yes or no.

1. In the beginning Cookie had:
   - a dish for water .... ○ yes ○ no
   - a purple bed .... ○ yes ○ no
   - a dish for food .... ○ yes ○ no
   - a yellow mouse .... ○ yes ○ no

2. Was Cookie happy to see Amy's surprise? .... ○ yes ○ no

3. Cookie
   - hissed at the new kitten .... ○ yes ○ no
   - scratched the new kitten .... ○ yes ○ no
   - swatted at the new kitten . ... ○ yes ○ no
   - chased the new kitten.................. ○ yes ○ no

4. The new kitten was afraid. .... ○ yes ○ no

5. Cookie decided to be the new kitten's friend. .... ○ yes ○ no

Skills: Using Picture Clues; Understanding Word Meaning

What Does It Mean?

Look at the pictures. Write the best word in each sentence.

sniffed	tasted	cried
licked	chased	swatted
purred	played	hissed

The kitten ____________ the flower.

Cookie ____________ at the kitten.

Cookie ____________ the kitten.

The little kitten ____________.

The kitten ____________ with the yarn.

Cookie ____________ the kitten's ear.

Skills: Making Connections; Using Prior Knowledge; Reading Animal Names

Animal Babies

Cut and paste to match the babies with the parents.
Write the names under the pictures.

paste

dog ____________

paste

horse ____________

paste

hen ____________

paste

cow ____________

paste

cat ____________

paste

rabbit ____________

Word Box

chick calf kit pup foal kitten

The Sound of k

Say the picture name. Write the letter **k** where you hear its sound.

 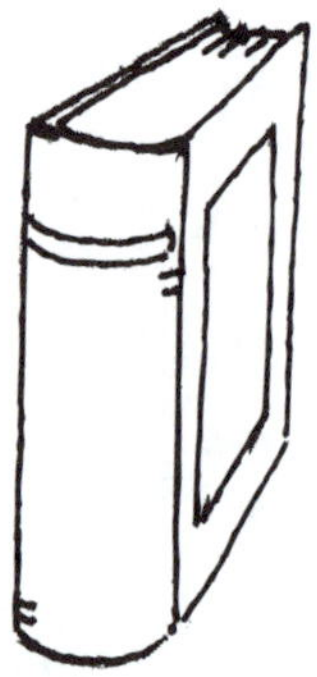 

__itten   __ook   __ey

  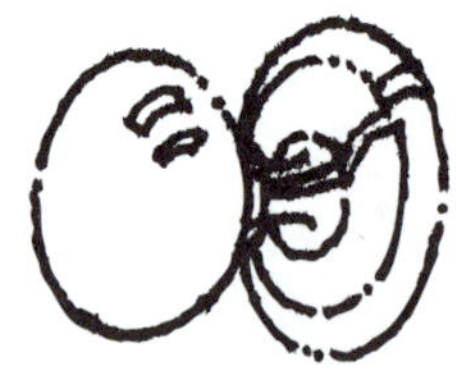

__angaroo   __oala   __oorknob

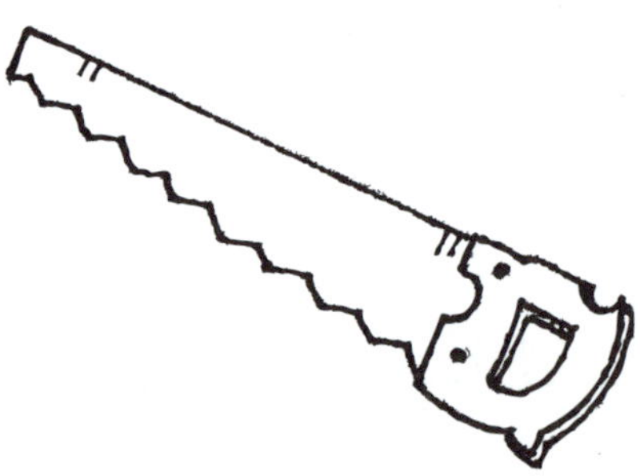 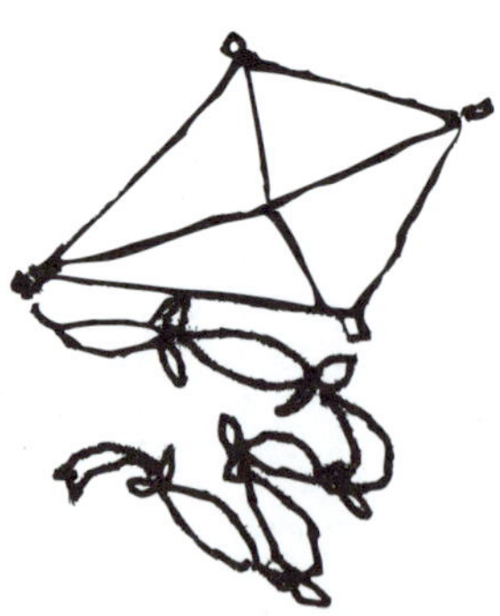 

__aw   __ite   __ing

Working with Word Families

ace

f + ace = __ __ __ __

l + ace = __ __ __ __

r + ace = __ __ __ __

pl + ace = __ __ __ __ __

sp + ace = __ __ __ __ __

tr + ace = __ __ __ __ __

Finish each picture. The words tell you what to do.

Make a sad face.

Draw the cars in the race.

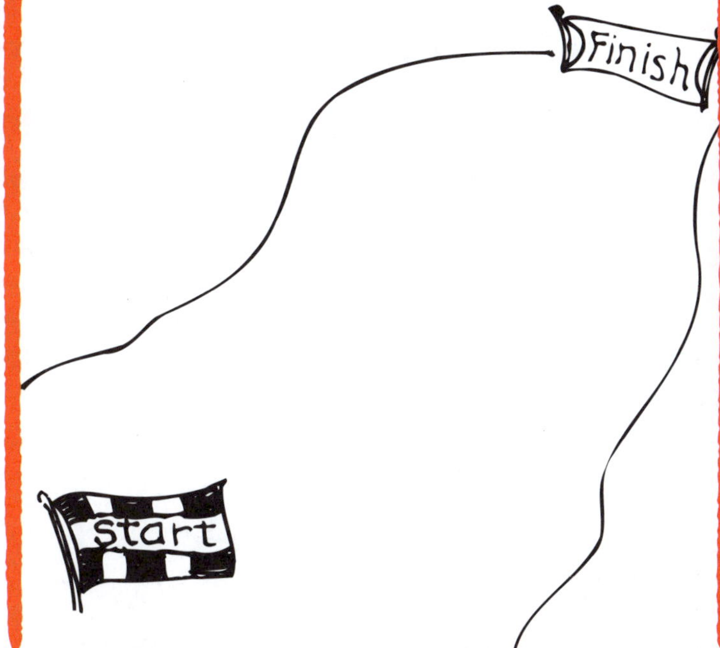

What Do You Think?

Fill in the circle in front of yes or no.

Can two cats be friends?	○ yes	○ no
Can two cats drive to the mall?	○ yes	○ no
Can two cats like the same toy?	○ yes	○ no
Can two cats chase one another?	○ yes	○ no
Can two cats lap the milk?	○ yes	○ no
Can two cats write a letter?	○ yes	○ no

Draw something two cats could really do.

The Missing Mitten

One day Tommy got ready to go outside. It was a cold, snowy day. Tommy put on his snow pants. He put on his jacket. He put on his long green stocking hat. His mother gave him a scarf to keep his neck warm. Next he pulled on his shiny yellow snow boots. They were new. Tommy couldn't wait to try them out. He was almost ready. All that he needed were his mittens.

Tommy reached into his jacket pocket. He pulled out one fuzzy blue mitten. One mitten? Where was the other mitten? Tommy looked all over. He looked like a marshmallow man stumbling around his room. Where was the missing mitten?

Tommy yelled to his mom, “Hey, Mom! I can only find one blue mitten. Will you help me find the other one?”

Tommy's mom came into his room. She took one look at Tommy and started to laugh.

Tommy frowned. "What are you laughing at?" he asked.

Tommy's mom pulled Tommy in front of the mirror. She pointed to his long stocking hat. Peeking out from under the hat was a blue thumb. A hat with a blue thumb?

Tommy reached up and pulled off the hat. There was the missing mitten!

What Did It Say?

Fill in the circle or write words to answer the questions.

1. What was missing?

   ○ hat ○ scarf ○ mitten

2. Who did the missing thing belong to?

   ○ Mom ○ Tommy ○ Dad

3. Where was the missing thing found?

   ____

Draw something that belongs to you that was missing.

Skills: Sequencing Story Details

Put It in Order

Color, cut, and paste. Show the order that Tommy put on his things before he went outside.

1	2
paste	*paste*
3	**4**
paste	*paste*
5	**6**
paste	*paste*

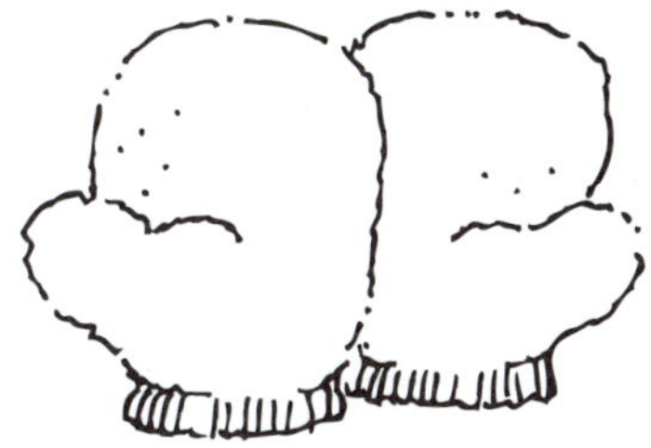

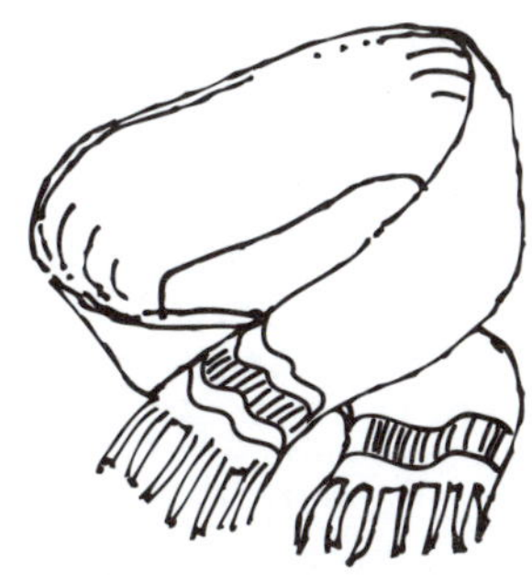

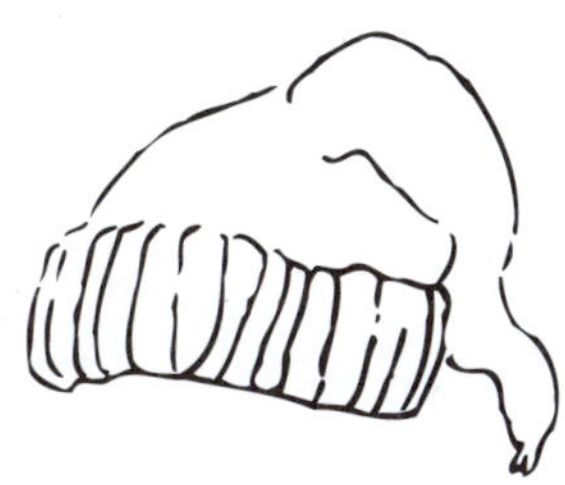

Whose Mittens?

Read the sentences. Then label the mittens. Use **'s** after the name of the owner.

Tommy has fuzzy blue mittens.

Molly has red mittens with blue stripes.

Baby has mittens with dog ears on them.

Dad has big mittens with metal clips.

Molly's mittens 

_______________ mittens 

_______________ mittens 

_______________ mittens 

Skills: Blending Words with the Word Part *–itten*; Completing Sentences

Working with Word Families

itten

Write the letters to make new words.

m + itten = _ _ _ _ _ _

k + itten = _ _ _ _ _ _

b + itten = _ _ _ _ _ _

wr + itten = _ _ _ _ _ _ _

Use the new words to complete these sentences.

1. The dog was ____________ by a flea.

2. My name is ______________ in this book.

3. The ____________ has soft fur and a nice meow.

4. The ____________ keeps my hand warm when it's cold.

Make Them the Same

Color the second mitten to match the first.
List three words that tell about the mittens.

1. ______________________
2. ______________________
3. ______________________

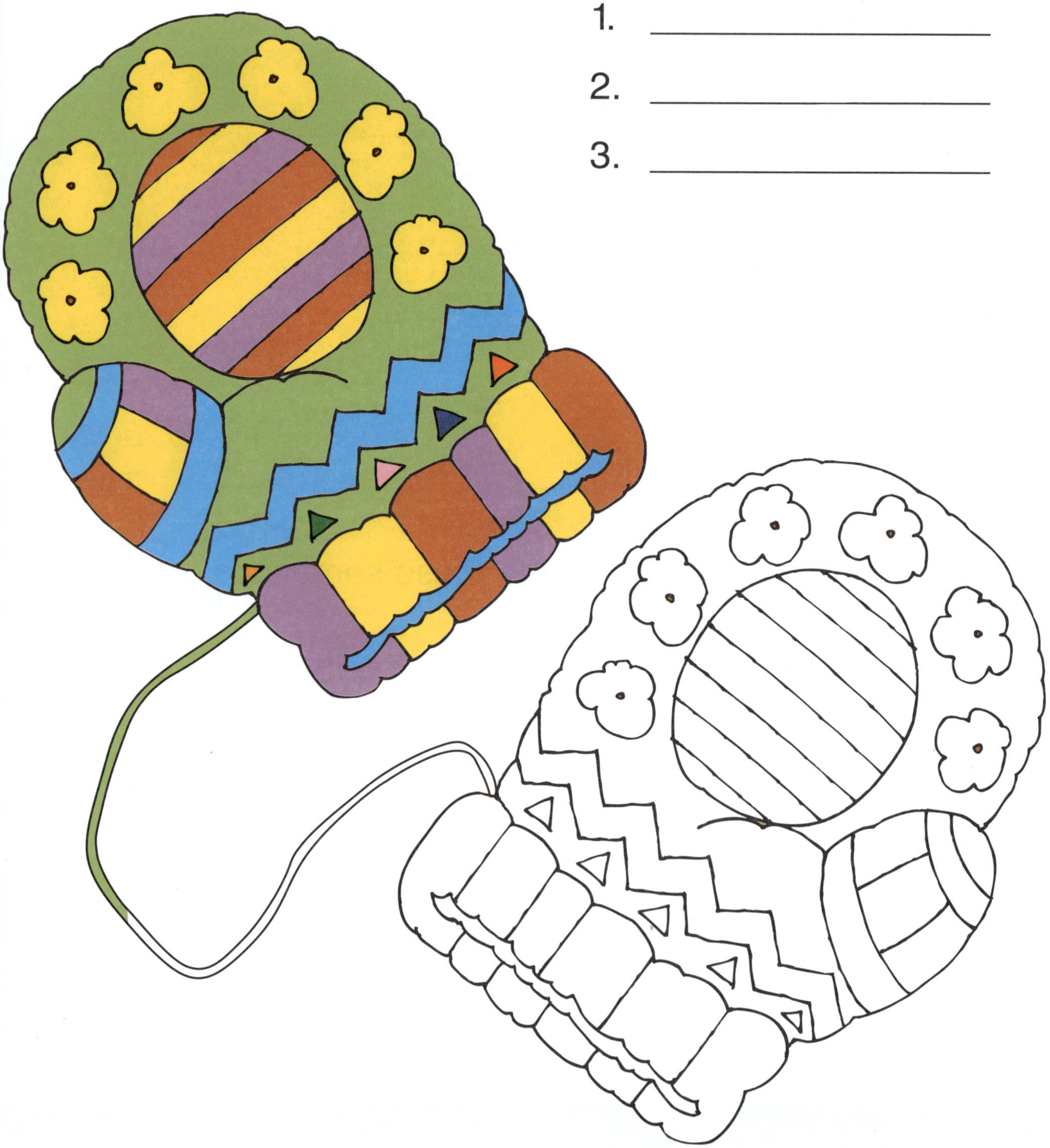

Color Crossword

Use color words to fill in the blanks of this crossword.

Across

3. What color is grape juice and an eggplant?
5. What color is the sky on a sunny day?
7. What color is soot from a fire?
8. What color are ripe tomatoes?
9. What color is the snow?
10. What color is hot chocolate?

Down

1. What color is a ripe pumpkin?
2. What color is a lemon?
3. What color is a cat's tongue?
4. What color is made from black and white?
6. What color is spinach?

black
blue
brown
gray
green
orange
pink
purple
red
white
yellow

A Mitten

Practice this page until you can read it with no mistakes.
Read it to an adult.

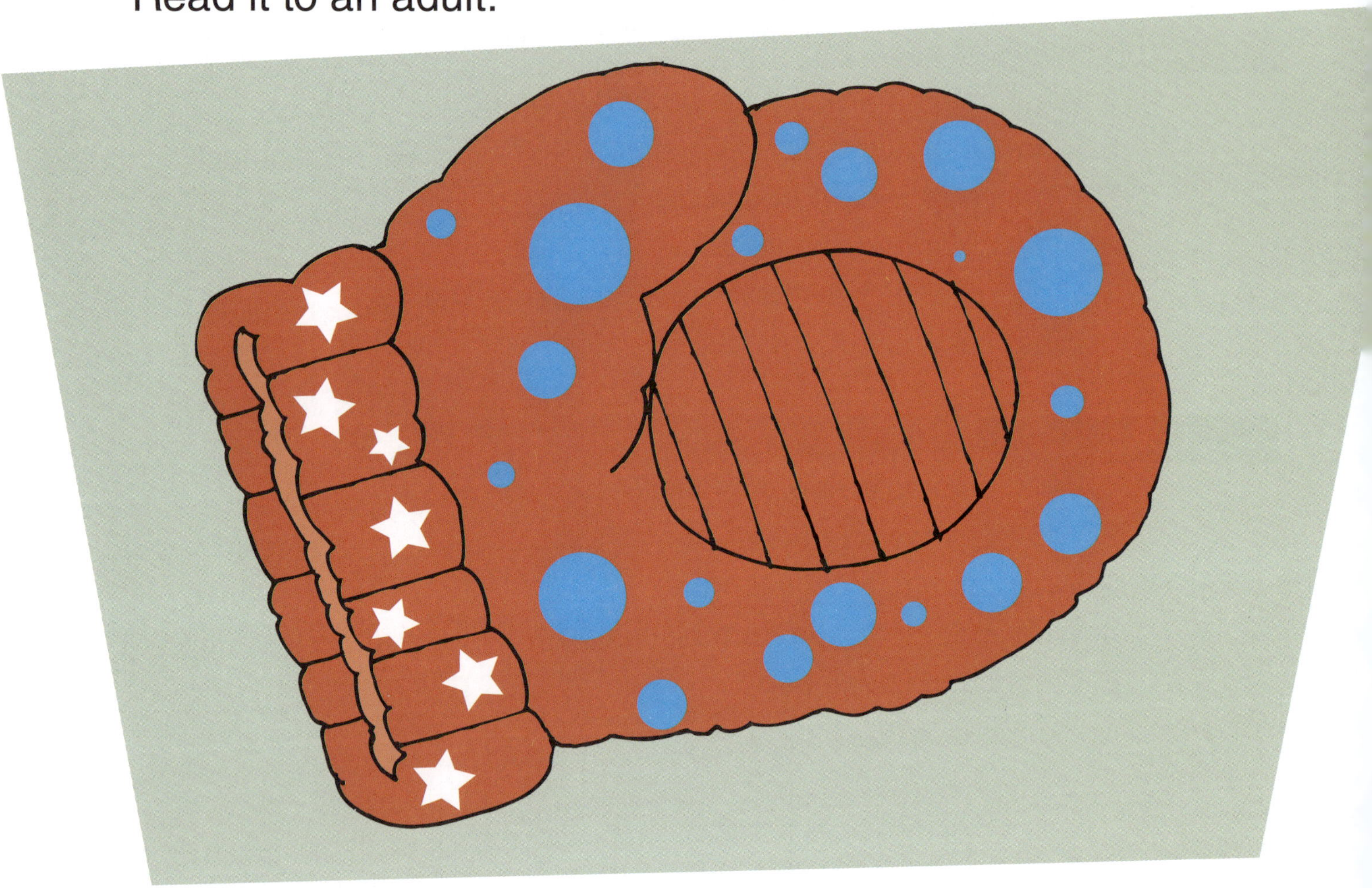

a mitten

a big mitten

a big red mitten

a big red mitten with blue dots

a big red mitten with blue dots and white stars

A New Neighbor

Peter looked down from his window. There was a big moving van next door. He watched as the man unloaded the van.

Peter wanted a new friend—a new friend who could play ball, ride bikes, and build things. Peter watched. The man unloaded a bike, a wagon, and a big bear.

Peter smiled. The new family must have a boy.

Just then a car pulled in behind the moving van. It was the new family. Peter watched. The family got out of the car. There was a boy! He had on a blue ball cap. Peter cheered. He watched the new family go inside their house.

Peter ran downstairs. He grabbed his ball and mitt. He ran next door. He knocked on the door. A man opened the door. Peter said, "Hi, I'm Peter. I live next door. Can your kid come out and play ball?"

The man smiled and said, "I'm glad to meet you, Peter. Sam was hoping to meet a new ball-playing friend. Sam loves to play ball. Sam can catch any ball you throw.

Peter smailed. He couldn't wait to meet Sam. It would be fun to have a pal next door.

The man called, "Sam, come meet our new neighbor. This is Peter. Peter, this is Samantha. We call her Sam."

Peter gulped. Samantha? That was a girl's name. His new neighbor was a girl! The kid with the blue ball cap was a girl? Peter didn't know what to do. He wanted a new friend. He wanted a pal who could play ball. He had thought that pal would be a boy.

Sam smiled at Peter. "Hi, Peter, want to play some catch?"

Peter nodded. He wondered if Sam could really catch. Her dad said she could catch anything.

Later Peter and Sam drank milk and ate cookies. Peter shook his head and smiled. "Sam, your dad was right. You can catch anything I throw. And you throw a mean fast ball, too. I'm glad that you moved next door to me."

After You Read

Practice pages 116 and 117. Use a different voice for each person that is talking. Read the pages to an adult.

What Did It Say?

Fill in the circle to show the answer.

1. How did Peter feel when he met Sam?
   ○ surprised ○ happy ○ mad

2. How did Peter feel after he played ball with Sam?
   ○ sad ○ glad ○ upset

3. Why did Peter think a new boy had moved in next door?
   ○ The mailman brought a letter.
   ○ His mother told him.
   ○ The moving man unloaded a bike and a wagon.

4. Why did Peter think that the new "boy" liked to play ball?
   ○ The new kid was holding a suitcase.
   ○ The moving man unloaded some bats.
   ○ The new kid was wearing a blue ball cap.

5. What did the new kid's dad boast?
   ○ He said that Sam was a good hitter.
   ○ He said that Sam was a good pitcher.
   ○ He said that Sam could catch any ball Peter threw.

Baseball Words

Use the words below to label the drawing.

baseball	mitt	ball cap	cleats
home plate	bat	backstop	batting glove

The Sound of gr

Color the pictures whose names begin with the sound that gr stands for.

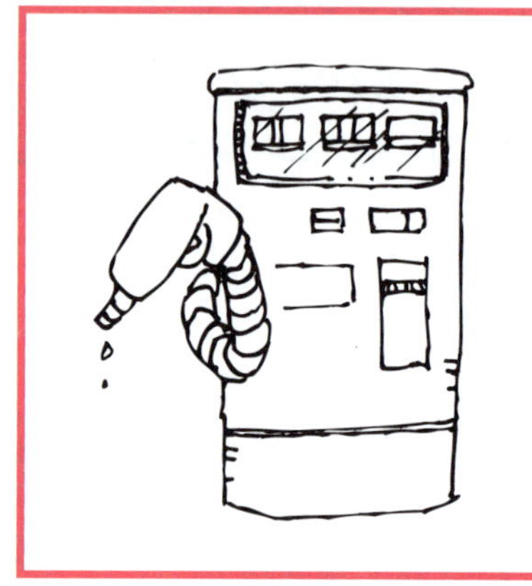

What grade are you in? ______________________________

Is the grass green? ______________________________

Are you ever grumpy? ______________________________

Skills: Sequencing Events

Draw a Story

Cut and paste the sentences in order. Then draw the story.

1

paste

2

paste

3

paste

4

paste

The ball was thrown.

Billy hit the ball hard.

Billy came to the plate.

It was a home run.

Skills: Blending Words in the –*ay* Family; Completing Sentences

Working with Word Families

ay

d + ay = ___ ___ ___

h + ay = ___ ___ ___

cl + ay = ___ ___ ___ ___

pl + ay = ___ ___ ___ ___

spr + ay = ___ ___ ___ ___ ___

str + ay = ___ ___ ___ ___ ___

Use the new words to complete these sentences.

1. The frog is made of ____________.
2. The cow sleeps on the ____________.
3. I want to go out and ____________.
4. ____________ the water on the flowers.
5. It's a bright sunny ____________.
6. That pup looks like a ____________.

George Washington's Barn

George Washington was an important man. Most people know him because he was the first president. Others, because he was a brave soldier.

But George Washington was an important farmer, too. He had a big farm in Virginia. He studied farming. He learned the best way to plant crops. He also learned the best way to harvest crops.

One of the crops that Mr. Washington planted was wheat. Kernels of wheat grow on stalks. When the wheat is ripe, the stalks are cut. The kernels are taken off the stalk. That's a hard job. The stalks are used as straw. The kernels are ground for making bread.

Mr. Washington had a plan. He wanted to make getting the wheat kernels easier. He built a special barn. The barn had 16 sides. It had a ramp up to the door. It was built on a hill so that it had a basement.

Workers cut the wheat. Then they spread it on the floor of the barn. Two mules walked up the ramp into the barn. They walked around and around on the wheat. The kernels of wheat came off the stalks. The kernels fell through holes in the floor to the basement. In the basement, workers swept up the wheat.

George Washington's plan worked. The mules did a good, fast job. Mr. Washington's wheat was ready for grinding. They could all have bread for dinner!

What Did It Say?

Think about what you read. Choose the best answer for each question. Look at the story again if you need to.

1. Why do most people know George Washington?
   - ◯ He was a brave soldier.
   - ◯ He was the first U.S. president.
   - ◯ He was a good farmer.

2. Where was George Washington's farm?
   - ◯ Washington, D.C.
   - ◯ New York
   - ◯ Virginia

3. How do you know farming was important to Mr. Washington?
   - ◯ He liked to eat bread.
   - ◯ He wanted to learn the best way to farm.
   - ◯ He fought in a war.

4. Why did Mr. Washington's barn make harvesting wheat easier?
   - ◯ It had a ramp so the workers didn't have to go up steps.
   - ◯ The mules did most of the work.
   - ◯ The workers didn't have to worry about rain.

What Does It Mean?

Read the information below. Use what you learn to fill in the blanks.

George Washington used five different kinds of fences on his farms.

- The **split rail fence** was a moveable fence. It could be laid in a zigzag pattern around trees.
- The **post and rail fence** was a permanent fence. It was used to make boundary lines.
- The **hurdle fence** was a small moveable fence. It was used to keep animals in an area for grazing.
- The **waddle fence** was a tightly woven split rail fence. It was used to pen birds and small animals.
- The **living hedge** was made of bushes. It was used between fields and pastures.

A split rail fence

Write the name of the fence that would be best.

1. A fence between your property and your neighbor's property ________________
2. A fence around the chicken yard ________________
3. A fence along a border with rocks and trees ________________
4. A fence to keep the sheep in one area of the pasture ________________

Reading a Map

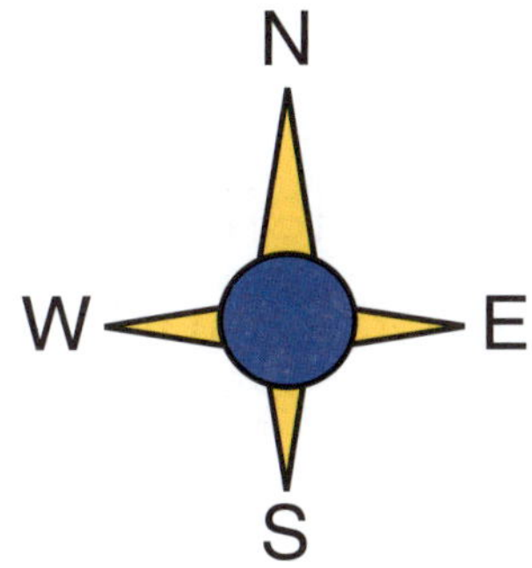

George Washington's big farm was called a plantation. This is a map of his plantation.

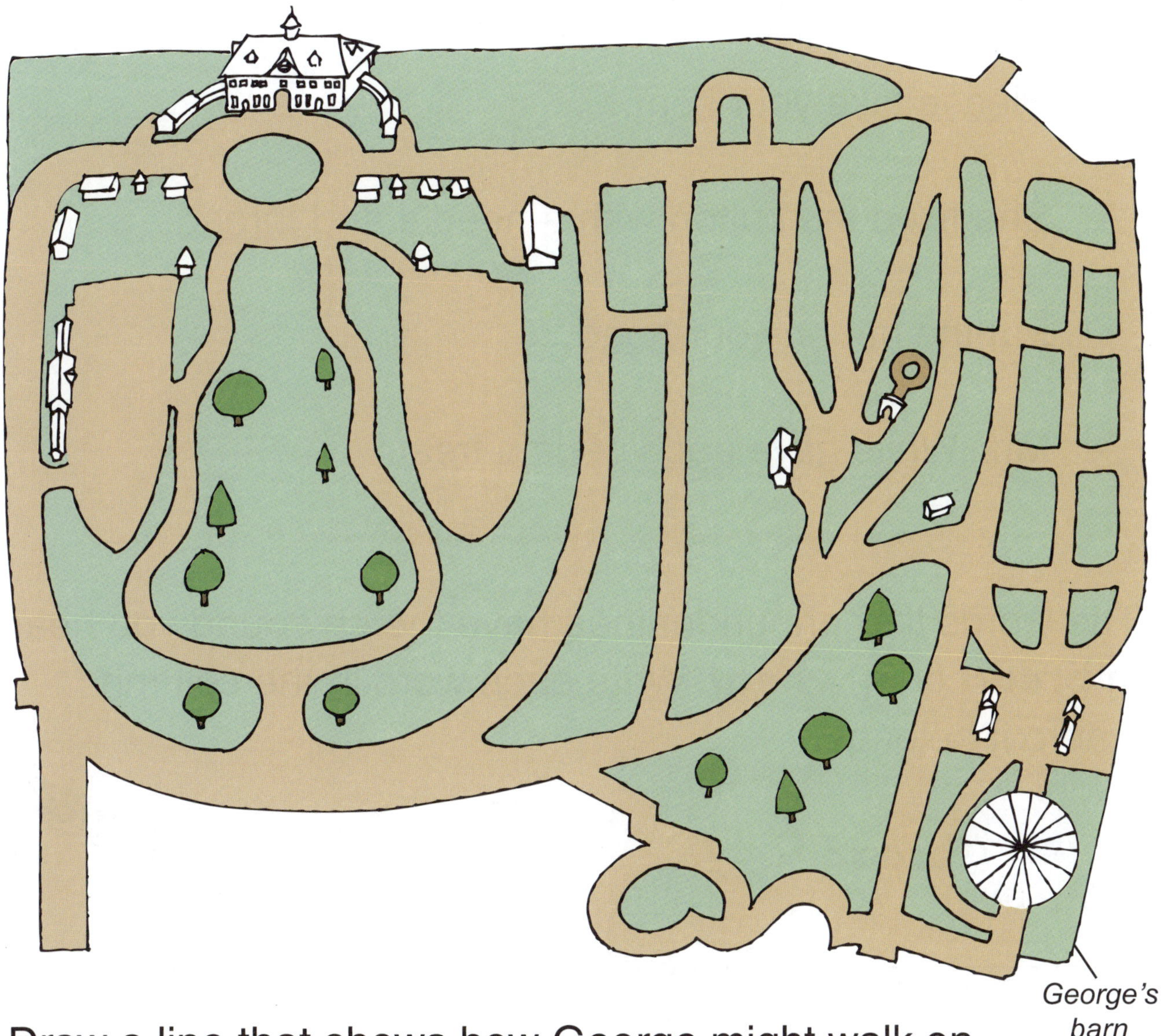

Draw a line that shows how George might walk on pathways from his house to his barn.

In which directions would he have to go? ______________

Skills: Reading a Words with Two Sounds of *ea;* Distinguishing the short and Long Sounds of *ea*

The Sounds of ea

The letters **ea** can stand for different sounds. Read the words and listen for two different **ea** sounds.

I am ready to plant the seeds.

Please take your seat.

She fixed the button with a needle and thread.

Put the hat on your head.

Mrs. White gave each of us a treat.

The words that are underlined have the **ea** sound you hear in **bread** or in **wheat**. Write each word in the column where it belongs.

bread 	**wheat** 
____________	____________
____________	____________
____________	____________
____________	____________

Skills: Sequencing

Put the Steps in Order

Cut and paste.

paste

paste

paste

paste

paste

paste

Make some bread.

Plant the wheat seeds.

Take the kernels off the stalk.

Water the seeds.

Cut the wheat stalks.

Grind the kernels into flour.

Skills: Blending Words in the –*alk* Family; Following Directions

Working with Word Families

alk

w + alk = ___ ___ ___ ___

st + alk = ___ ___ ___ ___ ___

t + alk = ___ ___ ___ ___

ch + alk = ___ ___ ___ ___ ___

Draw something you would see on a **walk** by a lake.

Draw a place where you cannot **talk**.

Skills: Seeing the Whole

Puzzle Page

Cut out the puzzle pieces. Put them together.

What do you have? ______________________________

paste	paste
paste	paste

Match the Opposites

Draw a line to match each pair of opposites.

plant	down
hard	slow
fast	harvest
up	less
more	easy

Draw something that is fast.

Draw something that is slow.

Tracking Form

Topic	Color in each page you complete.					
Dad and I	6	7	8	9	10	11
My Cocoon	14	15	16	17	18	19
Who Can Fix It?	24	25	26	27	28	29
Giant Tortoise	31	32	33	34	35	
Put It in the Pack	40	41	42	43		
An Ant on the Rug	48	49	50	51	52	
Who Lives in the Barn?	59	60	61	62	63	64
The Fix-It Man	70	71	72	73	74	75
What a Week!	78	79	80	81	82	83
Molly and Max	88	89	90	91	92	93
New Friends	97	98	99	100	101	102
The Missing Mitten	106	107	108	109	110	111
	112					
A New Neighbor	118	119	120	121	122	
George Washington's Barn	125	126	127	128	129	130
	131	132				

Answer Key

Checking your child's work is an important part of learning. It allows you to see what your child knows well and what areas need more practice. It also provides an opportunity for you to help your child understand that making mistakes is a part of learning.

When an error is discovered, ask your child to look carefully at the question or problem. Errors often occur through misreading. Your child can quickly correct these errors. Help your child with items she or he finds difficult.

The answer key pages can be used in several ways:

- Remove the answer pages and give the book to your child. Go over the answers as each story and the accompanying activity pages are completed.
- Leave the answer pages in the book and give the practice pages to your child one story unit at a time.

Page 6

What Did It Say?

Mark the things that the girl and her dad did in the story.

___ 1. They baked a cake.
_X_ 2. They raked the leaves.
___ 3. They read a book.
_X_ 4. They pulled the weeds.
___ 5. They washed the dog.
_X_ 6. They washed the car.

Draw something the dad did that the little girl did not do.

Drawings will vary.

8 ©2000 by Evan-Moor Corp. • Reading Practice at Home • EMC 4511

Page 7

Before and After

Color, cut, and paste to show how each thing looked before and after.

Before | After

The Lawn — We raked the leaves.

The Weeds — We pulled the weeds.

The Car — We washed the car.

©2000 by Evan-Moor Corp. • Reading Practice at Home • EMC 4511 9

Page 8

The Sound of p

Color the pictures that start with the sound p stands for.

poodle, pear, key, ball, penguin, purse, penny, cupcake, pizza, porcupine, pig, paint

10 ©2000 by Evan-Moor Corp. • Reading Practice at Home • EMC 4511

Page 9

This Is the Way to Wash a Car

Color the pictures. Cut and paste in order the directions for washing a car.

Get the car wet. | Wash off the dirt.

Rinse with clean water. | Dry off the car.

©2000 by Evan-Moor Corp. • Reading Practice at Home • EMC 4511 11

Page 10

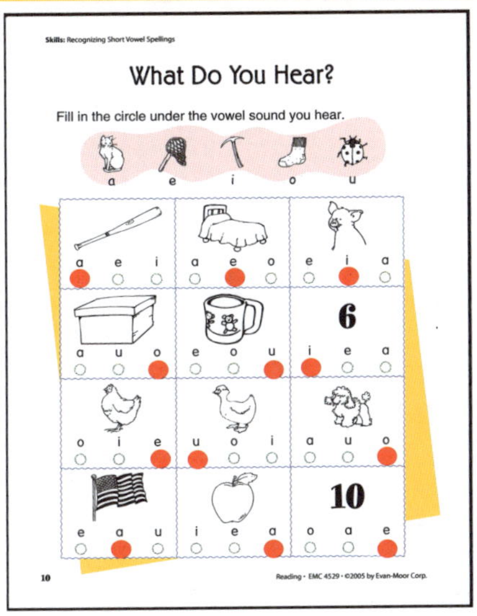
Skills: Recognizing Short Vowel Spellings

What Do You Hear?

Fill in the circle under the vowel sound you hear.

a e i o u

10 Reading • EMC 4529 • ©2005 by Evan-Moor Corp.

Page 11

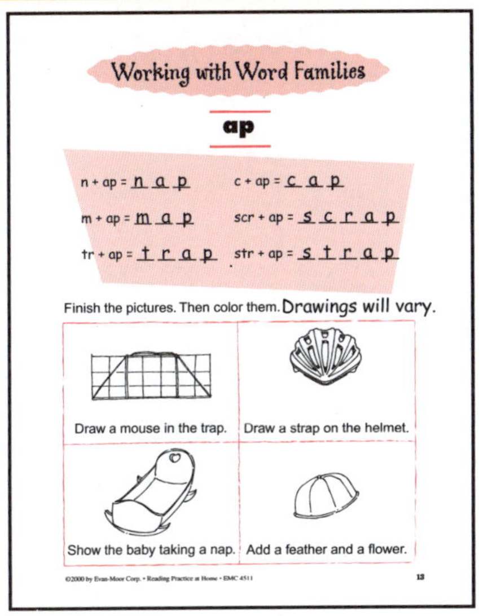
Working with Word Families

ap

n + ap = nap
c + ap = cap
m + ap = map
scr + ap = scrap
tr + ap = trap
str + ap = strap

Finish the pictures. Then color them. Drawings will vary.

Draw a mouse in the trap. | Draw a strap on the helmet.

Show the baby taking a nap. | Add a feather and a flower.

©2000 by Evan-Moor Corp. • Reading Practice at Home • EMC 4511 13

Page 14

Skills: Recalling Story Details; Understanding Opposites

What Did It Say?

Circle the words that tell about the cocoon and the sleeping bag.

cold (quiet) (warm) bright
loud busy (still) (dark)

Fill in the circle in front of the answer.

1. ○ It is warm here. ● It is cold here.
2. ○ It is dark here. ● It is bright here.
3. ● It is loud here. ○ It is quiet here.

14 Reading • EMC 4529 • ©2005 by Evan-Moor Corp.

Page 15

Opposites

Words like **loud** and **quiet** are called **opposites**. Draw a line to connect the opposites.

up	clean
high	busy
bright	down
still	slow
fast	dark
dirty	low

My hat is on.
My hat is off.

Draw pictures to show the **opposites**.

off empty
Drawings will vary.
on full

©2000 by Evan-Moor Corp. • Reading Practice at Home • EMC 4511 17

Page 16

Real or Make-Believe?

Circle **real** or **make-believe**.

real (make-believe)
(real) make-believe
(real) make-believe
real (make-believe)

Draw something about a butterfly that could be real.
Draw something about a butterfly that is make-believe.

Drawings will vary.

18 ©2000 by Evan-Moor Corp. • Reading Practice at Home • EMC 4511

Page 17

Put It in Order

Color, cut, and paste to put the pictures in order. Write about each picture.

1. Answers will vary.
2.
3.

©2000 by Evan-Moor Corp. • Reading Practice at Home • EMC 4511 19

Page 18

Working with Word Families

ill

h + ill = h i l l
f + ill = f i l l
ch + ill = c h i l l
dr + ill = d r i l l

Use the new words to complete these sentences.

1. Please fill my glass with milk.
2. I need a drill to fix the door.
3. He lives at the top of the hill.
4. If you go out in the cold you will get a chill.

20 ©2000 by Evan-Moor Corp. • Reading Practice at Home • EMC 4511

Page 19

Skills: Seeing the Whole; Writing a Description

Finish the Picture

Draw the other side of the butterfly. Then color the picture.

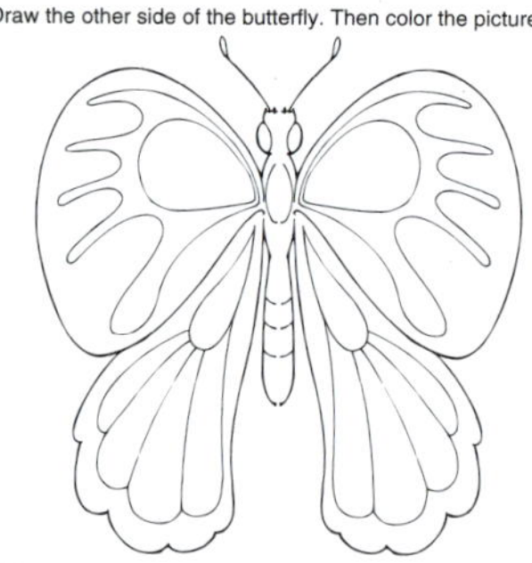

Write about the butterfly.

My butterfly Responses will vary.

©2005 by Evan-Moor Corp. • EMC 4529 • Reading 19

Page 24

Skills: Recalling Story Details; Matching Rhyming Words

What Did It Say?

Draw a picture of each thing. Then draw lines to tell who fixed it.

button	Mr. Snow
wheel	Sis
knob	Uncle Joe

Which thing could not be fixed quickly?

Words That Rhyme

Write the four words in the story that rhyme with **know**.

sew snow
Joe grow

24 Reading • EMC 4529 • ©2005 by Evan-Moor Corp.

Page 25

The Same Sound

Color the pictures that begin with the same sound as **button**.

©2000 by Evan-Moor Corp. • Reading Practice at Home • EMC 4511 27

Page 26

Working with Word Families

ar

j + ar = j a r
st + ar = s t a r
c + ar = c a r
b + ar = b a r
sc + ar = s c a r
f + ar = f a r

Use the new words to complete these sentences.

I will look at the star.
I can hang from the high bar.
I will put the bug in a jar.
I don't want to have a scar.

28 ©2000 by Evan-Moor Corp. • Reading Practice at Home • EMC 4511

Page 27

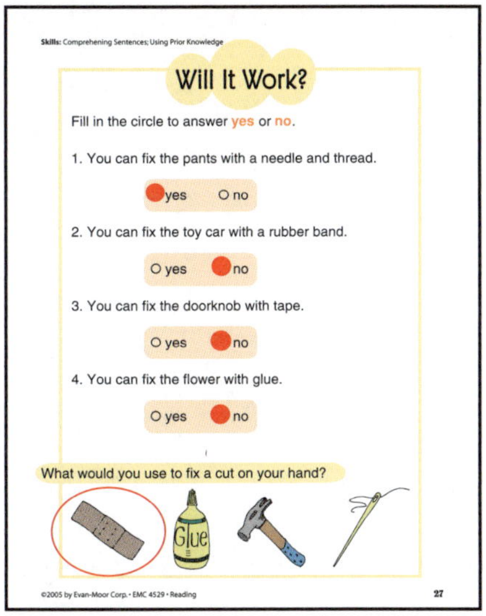

Skills: Comprehending Sentences; Using Prior Knowledge

Will It Work?

Fill in the circle to answer yes or no.

1. You can fix the pants with a needle and thread. ● yes ○ no
2. You can fix the toy car with a rubber band. ○ yes ● no
3. You can fix the doorknob with tape. ○ yes ● no
4. You can fix the flower with glue. ○ yes ● no

What would you use to fix a cut on your hand?

©2005 by Evan-Moor Corp. • EMC 4529 • Reading 27

Page 28

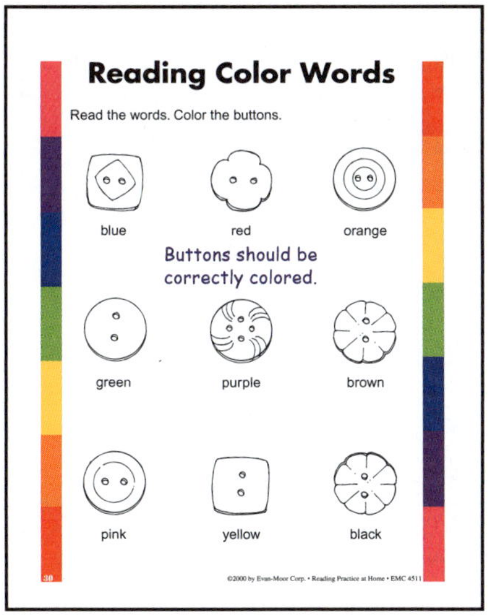

Reading Color Words

Read the words. Color the buttons.

blue red orange

Buttons should be correctly colored.

green purple brown

pink yellow black

©2000 by Evan-Moor Corp. • Reading Practice at Home • EMC 4511

Page 29

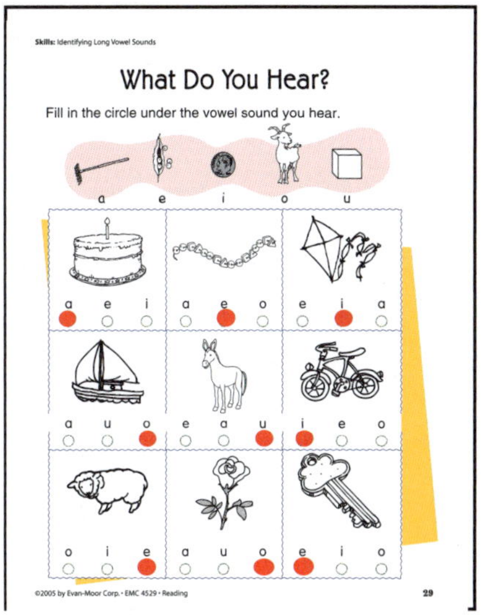

Skills: Identifying Long Vowel Sounds

What Do You Hear?

Fill in the circle under the vowel sound you hear.

a e i o u

©2005 by Evan-Moor Corp. • EMC 4529 • Reading 29

Page 31

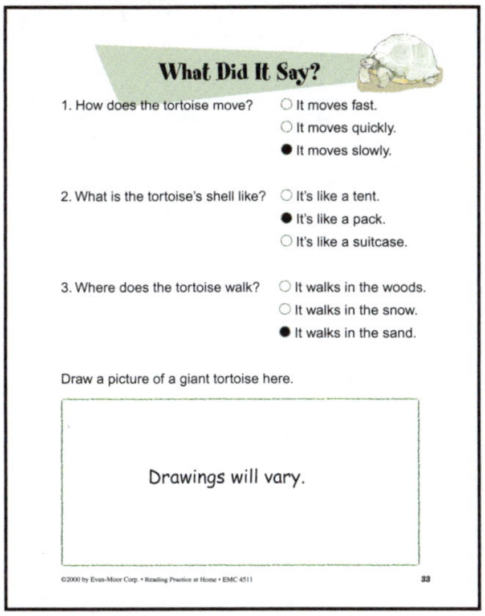

What Did It Say?

1. How does the tortoise move? ○ It moves fast. ○ It moves quickly. ● It moves slowly.
2. What is the tortoise's shell like? ○ It's like a tent. ● It's like a pack. ○ It's like a suitcase.
3. Where does the tortoise walk? ○ It walks in the woods. ○ It walks in the snow. ● It walks in the sand.

Draw a picture of a giant tortoise here.

Drawings will vary.

©2000 by Evan-Moor Corp. • Reading Practice at Home • EMC 4511 33

Page 32

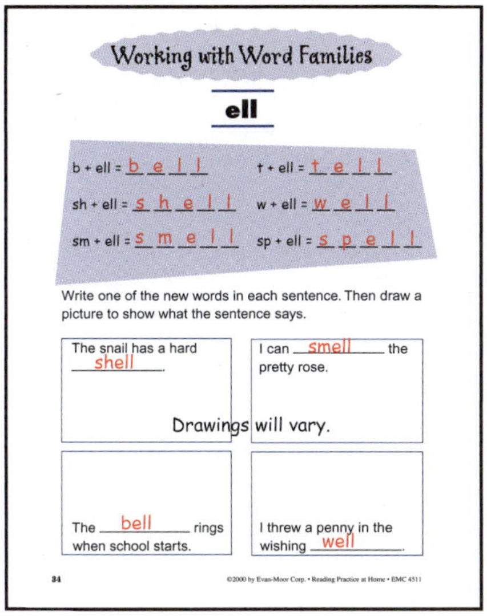

Working with Word Families

ell

b + ell = bell t + ell = tell

sh + ell = shell w + ell = well

sm + ell = smell sp + ell = spell

Write one of the new words in each sentence. Then draw a picture to show what the sentence says.

The snail has a hard shell.

I can smell the pretty rose.

Drawings will vary.

The bell rings when school starts.

I threw a penny in the wishing well.

34 ©2000 by Evan-Moor Corp. • Reading Practice at Home • EMC 4511

Page 33

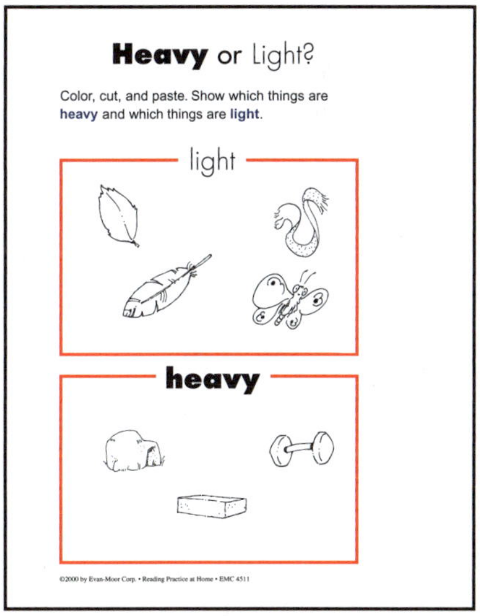

Heavy or Light?

Color, cut, and paste. Show which things are heavy and which things are light.

light

heavy

©2000 by Evan-Moor Corp. • Reading Practice at Home • EMC 4511

Page 34

Skills: Following Directions; Writing a Description

Cool, Man, Cool!

The tortoise wants to look cool. Can you color its shell in a special way? Add shoes and a hat.

Tell what the tortoise looks like.

Responses will vary.

34 Reading • EMC 4529 • ©2005 by Evan-Moor Corp.

Page 35

Skills: Using Prior Knowledge; Completing Sentences

In a Shell

Draw another animal that lives in a shell. Draw the place where it lives, too.

Drawings will vary.

I am a Responses will vary.

I live

©2005 by Evan-Moor Corp. • EMC 4529 • Reading 35

Page 40

What Did It Say?

1. Where is the little girl going?
2. How will the little girl carry her things?
3. What is the little girl's problem?
4. What does the little girl take out that she will need?

42 ©2000 by Evan-Moor Corp. • Reading Practice at Home • EMC 4511

Page 41

Working with Word Families

ack

b + ack = b a c k
p + ack = p a c k
cr + ack = c r a c k
qu + ack = q u a c k
sn + ack = s n a c k
tr + ack = t r a c k
s + ack = s a c k
r + ack = r a c k

Read the sentence in each box. Draw what it tells you to do.

Draw a dish with a crack. | Draw a snack you like to eat.

Drawings will vary.

Page 42

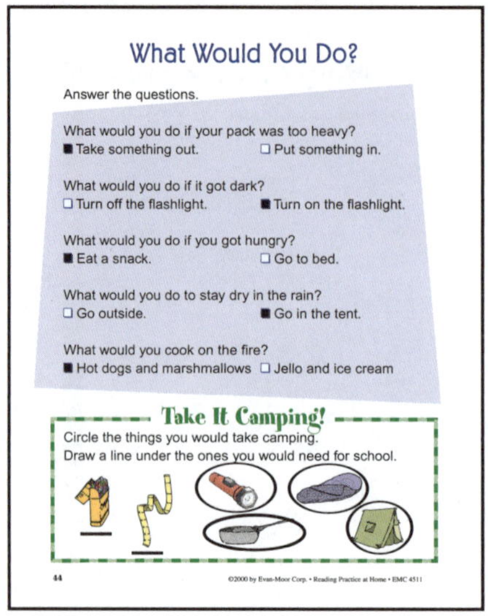

What Would You Do?

Answer the questions.

What would you do if your pack was too heavy?
■ Take something out. ☐ Put something in.

What would you do if it got dark?
☐ Turn off the flashlight. ■ Turn on the flashlight.

What would you do if you got hungry?
■ Eat a snack. ☐ Go to bed.

What would you do to stay dry in the rain?
☐ Go outside. ■ Go in the tent.

What would you cook on the fire?
■ Hot dogs and marshmallows ☐ Jello and ice cream

Take It Camping!

Circle the things you would take camping.
Draw a line under the ones you would need for school.

Page 43

Connect the Dots

Start with 1. Make something you might see on a camping trip.

Make a list of animals you might see on a camping trip.

Responses will vary.

Page 48

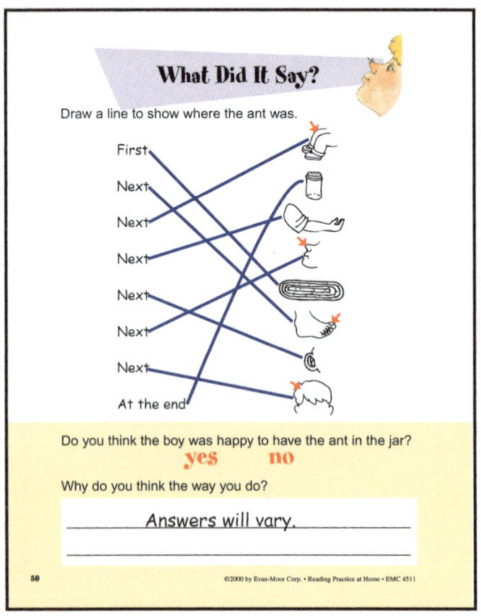

What Did It Say?

Draw a line to show where the ant was.

First
Next
Next
Next
Next
Next
Next
At the end

Do you think the boy was happy to have the ant in the jar?
yes no

Why do you think the way you do?

Answers will vary.

Page 49

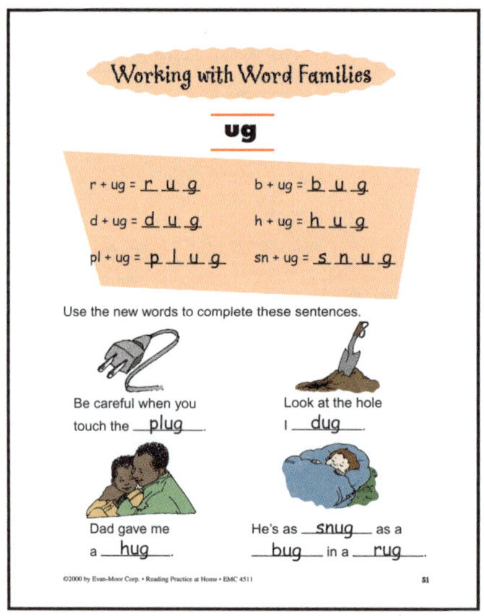

Working with Word Families

ug

r + ug = r u g
b + ug = b u g
d + ug = d u g
h + ug = h u g
pl + ug = p l u g
sn + ug = s n u g

Use the new words to complete these sentences.

Be careful when you touch the plug.

Look at the hole I dug.

Dad gave me a hug.

He's as snug as a bug in a rug.

Page 50

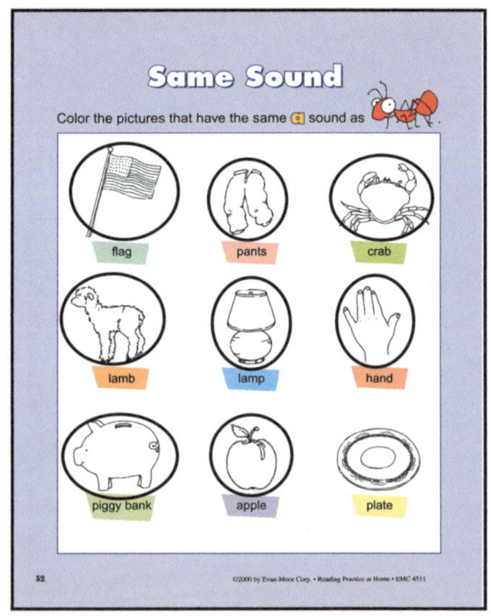

Same Sound

Color the pictures that have the same a sound as ant.

flag, pants, crab, lamb, lamp, hand, piggy bank, apple, plate

Page 51

What Does It Mean?

Cut and paste to label the picture.

hair, nose, ear, arm, knee, toe

Page 52

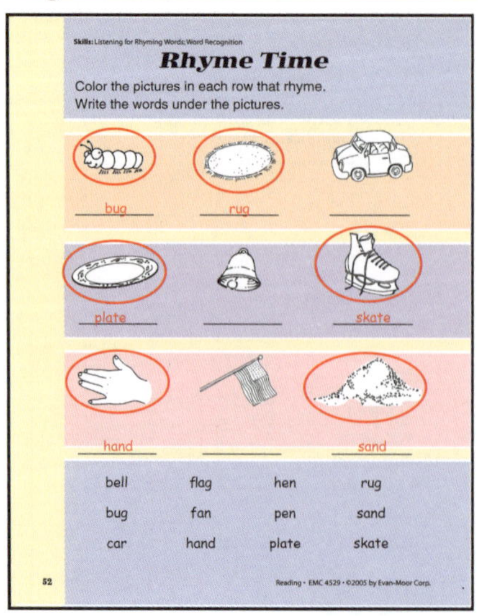

Rhyme Time

Color the pictures in each row that rhyme.
Write the words under the pictures.

bug rug
plate skate
hand sand

bell	flag	hen	rug
bug	fan	pen	sand
car	hand	plate	skate

Page 55

Who lives in the big red barn?

He's big and brown.
He shakes his head.
He stamps his foot.
He whinnies at me.

Who lives in the big red barn?

She flips her tail.
She wiggles her ears.
She nuzzles her calf.
She moos at me.

Page 56

Who lives in the big red barn?

She wears her winter coat.
She has a little bell.
She wakes her lamb.
She baas at me.

Who lives in the big red barn?

It flies from the roof.
It builds a small nest.
It sits on its eggs.
It peeps at me.

58 ©2000 by Evan-Moor Corp. • Reading Practice at Home • EMC 4511

Page 57

Who lives in the big red barn?

He stands by the door.
He runs to me.
He licks my hand.
He barks at me.

Who lives in the big red barn?

She laps the milk.
She licks her paws.
She feeds her kittens.
She purrs at me.

©2000 by Evan-Moor Corp. • Reading Practice at Home • EMC 4511 59

Page 58

Who lives in the big red barn?

It runs so fast.
It hides so well.
It nibbles food.
It squeaks at me.

Who lives in the big red barn?

60 ©2000 by Evan-Moor Corp. • Reading Practice at Home • EMC 4511

Page 59

Skills: Recalling Story Details

What Did It Say?

Fill in the circle under the correct answer.

1. Who builds a small nest? sheep / **swallow** / cat / mouse
2. Who nibbles food? sheep / swallow / cat / **mouse**
3. Who has a lamb? **sheep** / swallow / cat / mouse
4. Who flips her tail? horse / **cow** / dog / cat
5. Who licks a paw? horse / cow / dog / **cat**
6. Who barks? horse / cow / **dog** / cat
7. Who stamps a foot? **horse** / cow / dog / cat

©2005 by Evan-Moor Corp. • EMC 4529 • Reading 59

Page 60

Working with Word Families

ake

c + ake = cake
sn + ake = snake
r + ake = rake
sh + ake = shake
fl + ake = flake
br + ake = brake

Write the correct **-ake** word to finish each sentence.
Draw a picture to show what the sentence says.

I rake up the leaves.

A flake of snow is on my nose.

Drawings will vary.

62 ©2000 by Evan-Moor Corp. • Reading Practice at Home • EMC 4511

Page 61

Which Came First?

Cut and paste to put the animals in order.
Use the rhyme to help.

Who lives in the barn?

The horse, of course.
Wow, a cow!
My sheep is asleep.
Let's follow the swallow.
Not a frog! It's my dog.
Think of that. Mother cat!
The barn is a house for the mouse.

©2000 by Evan-Moor Corp. • Reading Practice at Home • EMC 4511

Page 62

What Does It Say?

Match the noise word to the animal that makes that noise.

baa, whinny, purr, squeak, chirp, moo, woof

Draw another animal here.
What noise does it make?
It says

Answers will vary.

Drawings will vary.

64 ©2000 by Evan-Moor Corp. • Reading Practice at Home • EMC 4511

Page 63

Think About It

Which animals live mainly on a farm?
Which animals live mainly in the jungle?
Write the names of the animals in the correct list.

goat, lion, elephant, chicken, horse, zebra, cow, monkey

On a farm	In the jungle
goat	lion
chicken	elephant
horse	zebra
cow	monkey

©2000 by Evan-Moor Corp. • Reading Practice at Home • EMC 4511 65

Page 64

The Big Red Barn

The picture should be correctly colored.

Read the color words. Then color the picture.

66 ©2000 by Evan-Moor Corp. • Reading Practice at Home • EMC 4511

Page 70

What Did It Say?

Fill in the circle by the correct answer.

1. Who did the boy call for help?
   ○ Mother ○ a friend ● Mr. Fix-It
2. What was wrong with the window?
   ○ It was stuck. ● It broke. ○ It needed washing.
3. Was Mr. Fix-It a good fixer?
   ○ No, he had to keep coming back.
   ○ Yes, he won a prize.
   ● Yes, he fixed everything.
4. Why do you think the boy called Mr. Fix-It the last time?
   ○ There were too many cookies in the jar.
   ○ The milk was going to spoil.
   ● Mr. Fix-It should have a treat.

Write an answer.
Who fixes things at your house?

Answers will vary.

72 ©2000 by Evan-Moor Corp. • Reading Practice at Home • EMC 4511

Page 71

Put It in Order

Mr. Fix-It will fix the wagon. Color the pictures.
Cut and paste to put them in the correct order.

1 2 3 4

The pictures should be colored.

©2000 by Evan-Moor Corp. • Reading Practice at Home • EMC 4511 73

Page 72

Can It Be Fixed?

Some things cannot be put back together. Write It can be fixed or It can't by each of the pictures below. Use your best handwriting.

It can't
It can
It can't
It can
It can
It can't

74 ©2000 by Evan-Moor Corp. • Reading Practice at Home • EMC 4511

Page 73

Working with Word Families

ink

p + ink = p i n k s + ink = s i n k
bl + ink = b l i n k dr + ink = d r i n k
shr + ink = s h r i n k th + ink = t h i n k

Draw a toy boat in a sink.	Draw a muddy pig that's pink.

Drawings will vary.

©2000 by Evan-Moor Corp. • Reading Practice at Home • EMC 4511 75

Page 74

More Than One

1 2 3 4 5

Add s to each word to mean more than one.
Then draw what the words say.

one door — two doors
one house — three houses
one bird — four birds
one flower — five flowers

Drawings will vary.

76 ©2000 by Evan-Moor Corp. • Reading Practice at Home • EMC 4511

Page 75

Rhyme Time

Color the pictures. Circle the words that rhyme.

house mouse cat
window sink ink
door bear chair
dish milk fish
cake snake hat

©2000 by Evan-Moor Corp. • Reading Practice at Home • EMC 4511 77

Page 78

Skills: Recalling Story Details

What Did I Have?

Fill in the circle under of the correct answer.

1. What did I have on Tuesday?
   turkey ○ tuna ● soup ○
2. What did I have on Friday?
   waffles ○ muffins ○ fries ●
3. What did I have on Sunday?
   soup ● soda ○ turkey ○
4. What did I have on Monday?
   waffles ○ fries ○ muffins ●
5. What did I have on Saturday?
   soup ○ soda ● tuna ○

78 Reading • EMC 4529 • ©2005 by Evan-Moor Corp.

Page 79

My Favorite Foods

Rewrite the story. Draw or write what you would like to eat each day beside the name of the day. Then read the story using your foods.

Monday
I have — Answers will vary.

Tuesday
I have

Wednesday
I have

Thursday
I have

Friday
I have

Saturday
I have

Sunday
I have

©2000 by Evan-Moor Corp. • Reading Practice at Home • EMC 4511 81

Page 80

Working with Word Families

unch

l + unch = l u n c h m + unch = m u n c h
b + unch = b u n c h p + unch = p u n c h
cr + unch = c r u n c h

Circle each word from the -unch family in the story below. Draw pictures to show the animals eating.

See the goats? They like to eat. Munch, Munch, Hay for lunch.	See the squirrels? They like to eat. Munch, Munch, Hear the crunch.	See the monkeys? They like to eat. Munch, Munch, What a bunch.

Drawings will vary.

82 ©2000 by Evan-Moor Corp. • Reading Practice at Home • EMC 4511

Page 81

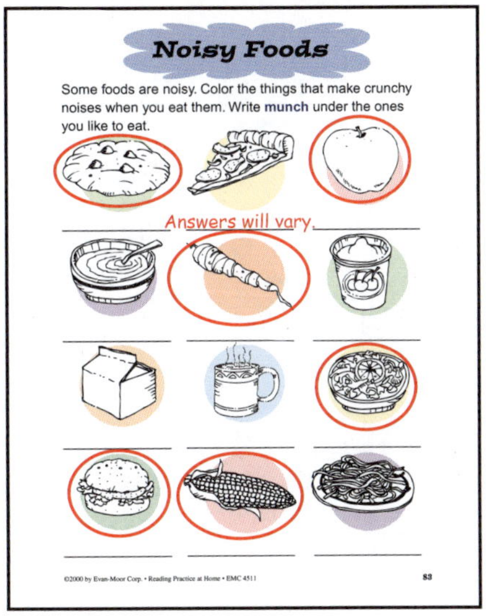
Noisy Foods

Some foods are noisy. Color the things that make crunchy noises when you eat them. Write **munch** under the ones you like to eat.

Answers will vary.

©2000 by Evan-Moor Corp. • Reading Practice at Home • EMC 4511 83

Page 82

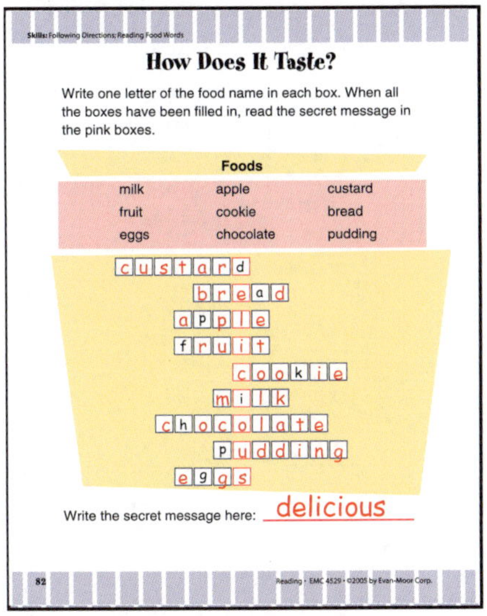
Skills: Following Directions; Reading Food Words

How Does It Taste?

Write one letter of the food name in each box. When all the boxes have been filled in, read the secret message in the pink boxes.

Foods		
milk	apple	custard
fruit	cookie	bread
eggs	chocolate	pudding

custard
bread
apple
fruit
cookie
milk
chocolate
pudding
eggs

Write the secret message here: delicious

82 Reading • EMC 4529 • ©2005 by Evan-Moor Corp.

Page 83

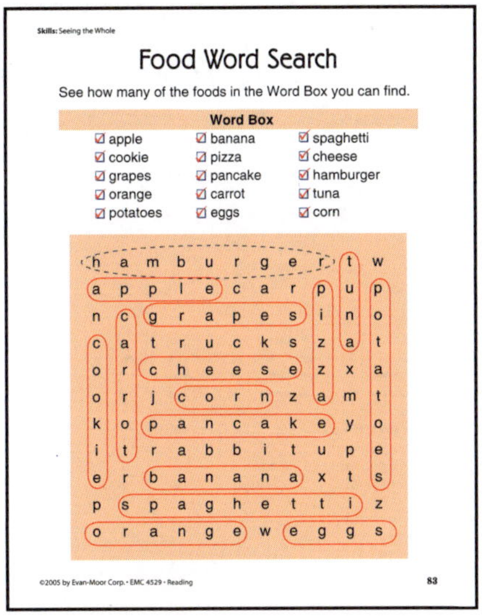
Skills: Seeing the Whole

Food Word Search

See how many of the foods in the Word Box you can find.

Word Box		
☑ apple	☑ banana	☑ spaghetti
☑ cookie	☑ pizza	☑ cheese
☑ grapes	☑ pancake	☑ hamburger
☑ orange	☑ carrot	☑ tuna
☑ potatoes	☑ eggs	☑ corn

h a m b u r g e r t w
a p p l e c a r p u p
n c g r a p e s i n o
c a t r u c k s z a t
o r c h e e s e z x a
o r j c o r n z a m t
k o p a n c a k e y o
i t r a b b i t u p e
e r b a n a n a x t s
p s p a g h e t t i z
o r a n g e w e g g s

©2005 by Evan-Moor Corp. • EMC 4529 • Reading 83

Page 88

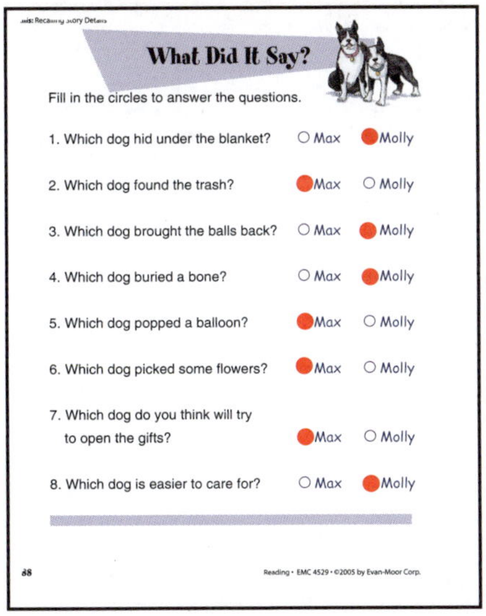
Skill: Recalling Story Details

What Did It Say?

Fill in the circles to answer the questions.

1. Which dog hid under the blanket? ○ Max ● Molly
2. Which dog found the trash? ● Max ○ Molly
3. Which dog brought the balls back? ○ Max ● Molly
4. Which dog buried a bone? ○ Max ● Molly
5. Which dog popped a balloon? ● Max ○ Molly
6. Which dog picked some flowers? ● Max ○ Molly
7. Which dog do you think will try to open the gifts? ● Max ○ Molly
8. Which dog is easier to care for? ○ Max ● Molly

88 Reading • EMC 4529 • ©2005 by Evan-Moor Corp.

Page 89

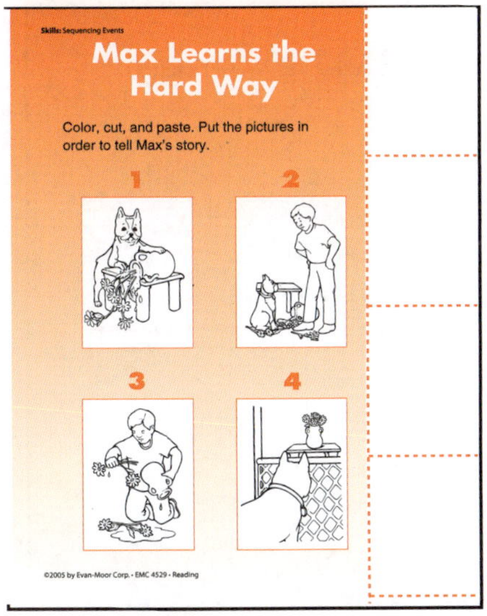
Skills: Sequencing Events

Max Learns the Hard Way

Color, cut, and paste. Put the pictures in order to tell Max's story.

1 2 3 4

©2005 by Evan-Moor Corp. • EMC 4529 • Reading

Page 90

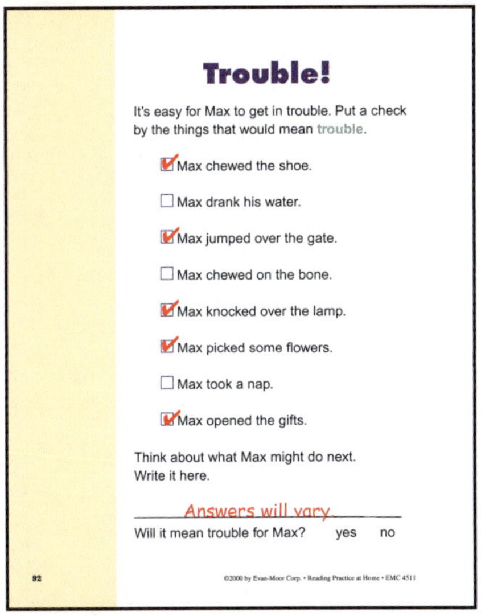
Trouble!

It's easy for Max to get in trouble. Put a check by the things that would mean trouble.

- ☑ Max chewed the shoe.
- ☐ Max drank his water.
- ☑ Max jumped over the gate.
- ☐ Max chewed on the bone.
- ☑ Max knocked over the lamp.
- ☑ Max picked some flowers.
- ☐ Max took a nap.
- ☑ Max opened the gifts.

Think about what Max might do next. Write it here.

Answers will vary.

Will it mean trouble for Max? yes no

92 ©2000 by Evan-Moor Corp. • Reading Practice at Home • EMC 4511

Page 91

Working with Word Families

one

b + one = b o n e
c + one = c o n e
ph + one = p h o n e
st + one = s t o n e
thr + one = t h r o n e
z + one = z o n e

Write the words to label the pictures.

phone cone
throne bone
stone end zone

©2000 by Evan-Moor Corp. • Reading Practice at Home • EMC 4511 92

Page 92

What's at the End?

Write the letter that stands for the sound you hear at the end of each word.

do**g** doo**r**
ba**g** boo**t**
cu**p** ja**r**
tu**b** ma**n**
ca**t** bo**x**

94 ©2000 by Evan-Moor Corp. • Reading Practice at Home • EMC 4511

Page 93

Skills: Following Directions; Seeing the Whole; Writing a Comparison

Draw a Pup

Follow the steps to draw a puppy.

Responses will vary.

How is the pup like Max?

Responses will vary.

How is the pup different from Max?

©2005 by Evan-Moor Corp. • EMC 4529 • Reading 93

Page 97

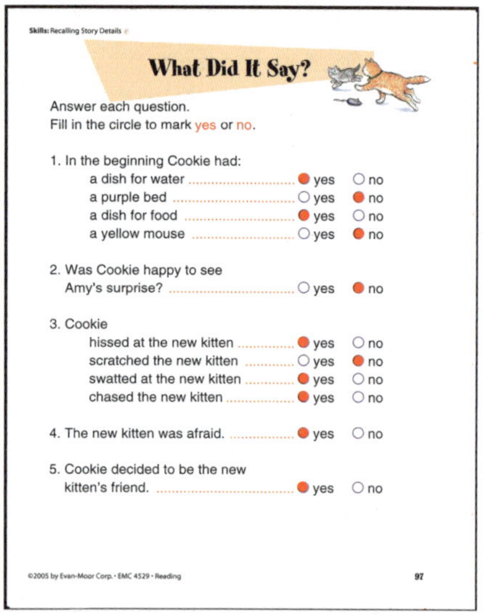

Skills: Recalling Story Details

What Did It Say?

Answer each question.
Fill in the circle to mark yes or no.

1. In the beginning Cookie had:
   - a dish for water ● yes ○ no
   - a purple bed ○ yes ● no
   - a dish for food ● yes ○ no
   - a yellow mouse ○ yes ● no
2. Was Cookie happy to see Amy's surprise? ○ yes ● no
3. Cookie
   - hissed at the new kitten ● yes ○ no
   - scratched the new kitten ○ yes ● no
   - swatted at the new kitten ● yes ○ no
   - chased the new kitten ● yes ○ no
4. The new kitten was afraid. ● yes ○ no
5. Cookie decided to be the new kitten's friend. ● yes ○ no

©2005 by Evan-Moor Corp. • EMC 4529 • Reading 97

Page 98

What Does It Mean?

Look at the pictures. Write the best word in each sentence.

sniffed	tasted	cried
licked	chased	swatted
purred	played	hissed

The kitten sniffed the flower.

Cookie hissed at the kitten.

Cookie chased the kitten.

The little kitten cried.

The kitten played with the yarn.

Cookie licked the kitten's ear.

100 ©2000 by Evan-Moor Corp. • Reading Practice at Home • EMC 4511

Page 99

Skills: Making Connections; Using Prior Knowledge; Reading Animal Names

Animal Babies

Cut and paste to match the babies with the parents.
Write the names under the pictures.

dog — pup; horse — foal

hen — chick; cow — calf

cat — kitten; rabbit — kit

Word Box: chick calf kit pup foal kitten

© Evan-Moor Corp. • EMC 4529 • Reading 99

Page 100

Skills: Listening for the /k/ Sound; Adding the Letter k to Complete Words

The Sound of k

Say the picture name. Write the letter k where you hear its sound.

kitten __ook key

kangaroo koala __oorknob

__aw kite king

100 Reading • EMC 4529 • ©2005 by Evan-Moor Corp.

Page 101

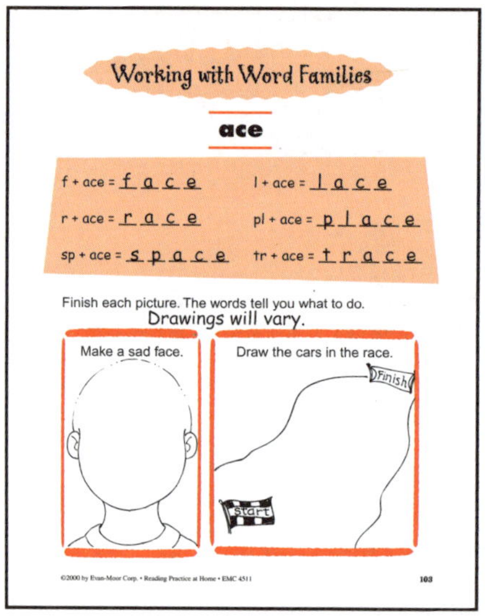

Working with Word Families

ace

f + ace = face   l + ace = lace

r + ace = race   pl + ace = place

sp + ace = space   tr + ace = trace

Finish each picture. The words tell you what to do.
Drawings will vary.

Make a sad face.   Draw the cars in the race.

Finish   Start

©2000 by Evan-Moor Corp. • Reading Practice at Home • EMC 4511 103

Page 102

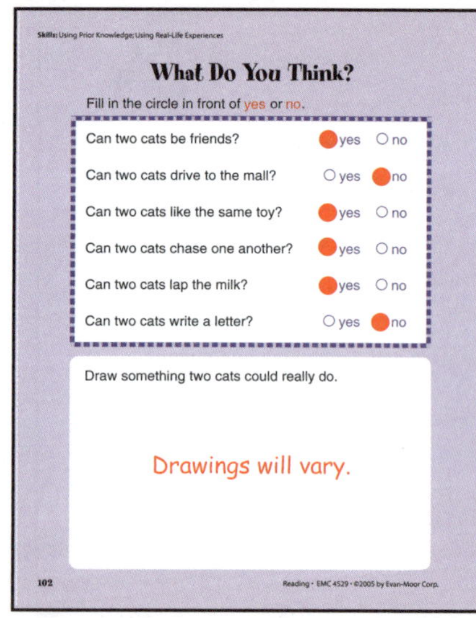

Skills: Using Prior Knowledge; Using Real-Life Experiences

What Do You Think?

Fill in the circle in front of yes or no.

- Can two cats be friends? ● yes ○ no
- Can two cats drive to the mall? ○ yes ● no
- Can two cats like the same toy? ● yes ○ no
- Can two cats chase one another? ● yes ○ no
- Can two cats lap the milk? ● yes ○ no
- Can two cats write a letter? ○ yes ● no

Draw something two cats could really do.

Drawings will vary.

102 Reading • EMC 4529 • ©2005 by Evan-Moor Corp.

Page 106

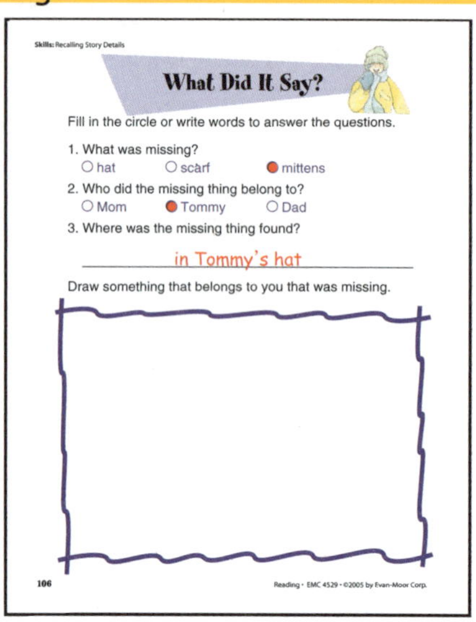

Skills: Recalling Story Details

What Did It Say?

Fill in the circle or write words to answer the questions.

1. What was missing?
   ○ hat ○ scarf ● mittens
2. Who did the missing thing belong to?
   ○ Mom ● Tommy ○ Dad
3. Where was the missing thing found?
   in Tommy's hat

Draw something that belongs to you that was missing.

106 Reading • EMC 4529 • ©2005 by Evan-Moor Corp.

Page 107

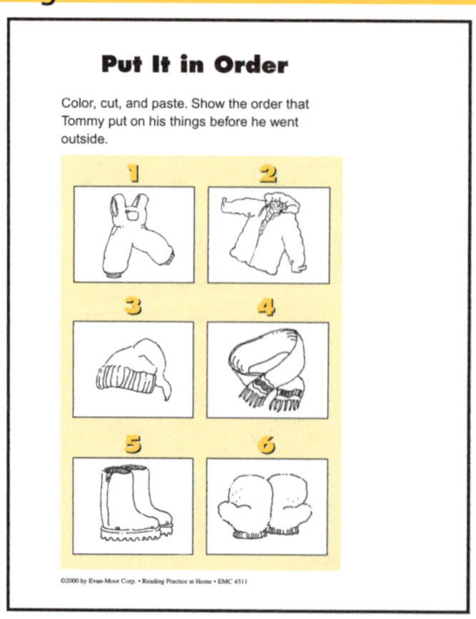

Put It in Order

Color, cut, and paste. Show the order that Tommy put on his things before he went outside.

1 2 3 4 5 6

©2000 by Evan-Moor Corp. • Reading Practice at Home • EMC 4511

Page 108

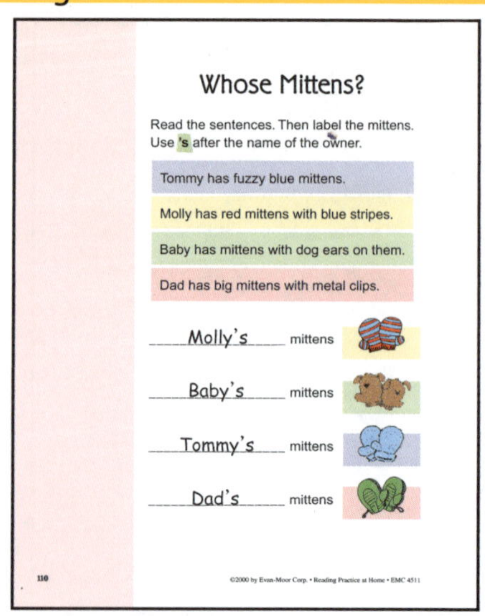

Whose Mittens?

Read the sentences. Then label the mittens.
Use 's after the name of the owner.

- Tommy has fuzzy blue mittens.
- Molly has red mittens with blue stripes.
- Baby has mittens with dog ears on them.
- Dad has big mittens with metal clips.

Molly's mittens

Baby's mittens

Tommy's mittens

Dad's mittens

110 ©2000 by Evan-Moor Corp. • Reading Practice at Home • EMC 4511

Page 109

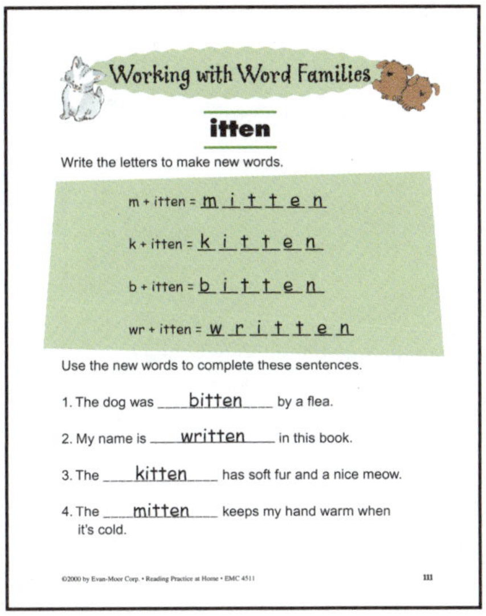
Working with Word Families

itten

Write the letters to make new words.

m + itten = m i t t e n

k + itten = k i t t e n

b + itten = b i t t e n

wr + itten = w r i t t e n

Use the new words to complete these sentences.

1. The dog was bitten by a flea.
2. My name is written in this book.
3. The kitten has soft fur and a nice meow.
4. The mitten keeps my hand warm when it's cold.

©2000 by Evan-Moor Corp. • Reading Practice at Home • EMC 4511 111

Page 110

Skills: Writing Descriptive Words

Make Them the Same

Color the second mitten to match the first.
List three words that tell about the mittens.

1. Responses will vary.
2.
3.

110 Reading • EMC 4529 • ©2005 by Evan-Moor Corp.

Page 111

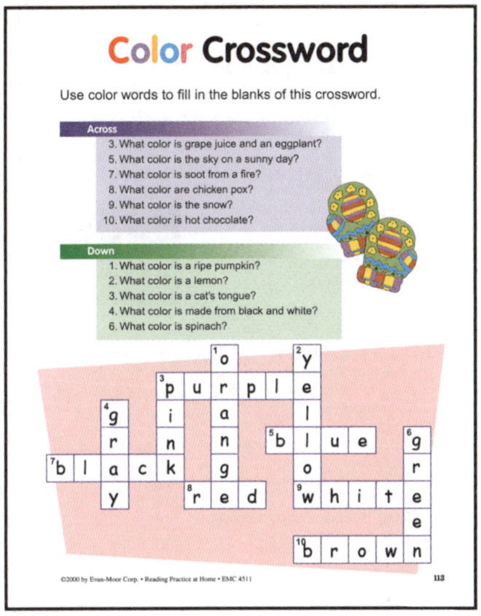
Color Crossword

Use color words to fill in the blanks of this crossword.

Across
3. What color is grape juice and an eggplant?
5. What color is the sky on a sunny day?
7. What color is soot from a fire?
8. What color are chicken pox?
9. What color is the snow?
10. What color is hot chocolate?

Down
1. What color is a ripe pumpkin?
2. What color is a lemon?
3. What color is a cat's tongue?
4. What color is made from black and white?
6. What color is spinach?

Across: 3 purple, 5 blue, 7 black, 8 red, 9 white, 10 brown
Down: 1 orange, 2 yellow, 3 pink, 4 gray, 6 green

©2000 by Evan-Moor Corp. • Reading Practice at Home • EMC 4511 113

Page 112

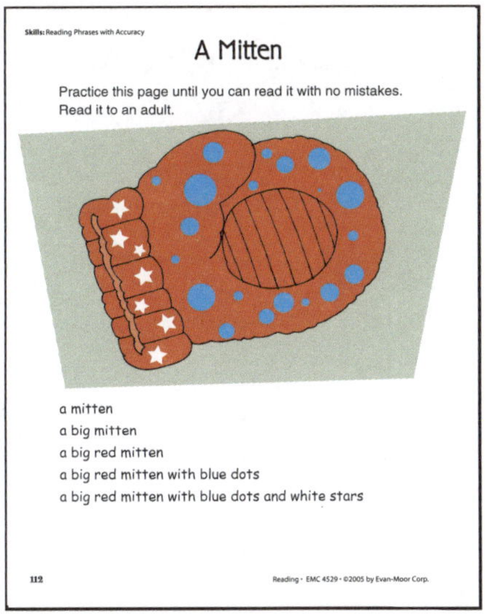
Skills: Reading Phrases with Accuracy

A Mitten

Practice this page until you can read it with no mistakes. Read it to an adult.

a mitten
a big mitten
a big red mitten
a big red mitten with blue dots
a big red mitten with blue dots and white stars

112 Reading • EMC 4529 • ©2005 by Evan-Moor Corp.

Page 118

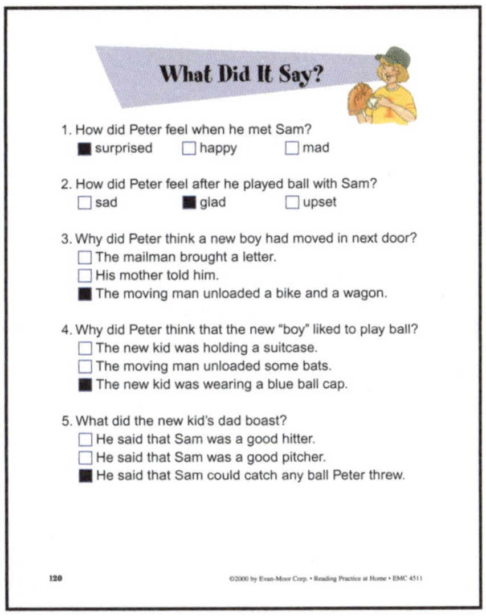
What Did It Say?

1. How did Peter feel when he met Sam?
■ surprised ☐ happy ☐ mad
2. How did Peter feel after he played ball with Sam?
☐ sad ■ glad ☐ upset
3. Why did Peter think a new boy had moved in next door?
☐ The mailman brought a letter.
☐ His mother told him.
■ The moving man unloaded a bike and a wagon.
4. Why did Peter think that the new "boy" liked to play ball?
☐ The new kid was holding a suitcase.
☐ The moving man unloaded some bats.
■ The new kid was wearing a blue ball cap.
5. What did the new kid's dad boast?
☐ He said that Sam was a good hitter.
☐ He said that Sam was a good pitcher.
■ He said that Sam could catch any ball Peter threw.

120 ©2000 by Evan-Moor Corp. • Reading Practice at Home • EMC 4511

Page 119

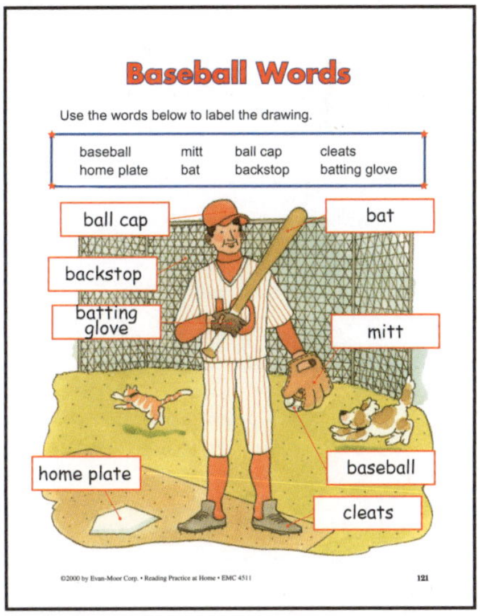
Baseball Words

Use the words below to label the drawing.

baseball, mitt, ball cap, cleats, home plate, bat, backstop, batting glove

©2000 by Evan-Moor Corp. • Reading Practice at Home • EMC 4511 121

Page 120

The Sound of gr

Color the pictures whose names begin with the sound that gr stands for.

What grade are you in? Answers will vary.

Is the grass green?

Are you ever grumpy?

122 ©2000 by Evan-Moor Corp. • Reading Practice at Home • EMC 4511

Page 121

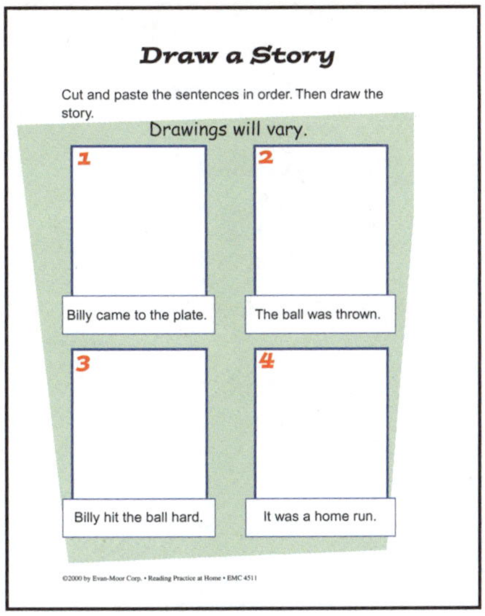
Draw a Story

Cut and paste the sentences in order. Then draw the story.

Drawings will vary.

1 Billy came to the plate.
2 The ball was thrown.
3 Billy hit the ball hard.
4 It was a home run.

©2000 by Evan-Moor Corp. • Reading Practice at Home • EMC 4511

Page 122

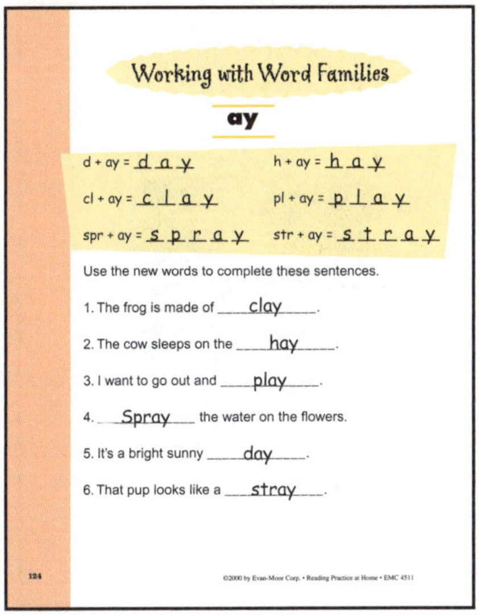
Working with Word Families

ay

d + ay = d a y
h + ay = h a y
cl + ay = c l a y
pl + ay = p l a y
spr + ay = s p r a y
str + ay = s t r a y

Use the new words to complete these sentences.

1. The frog is made of clay.
2. The cow sleeps on the hay.
3. I want to go out and play.
4. Spray the water on the flowers.
5. It's a bright sunny day.
6. That pup looks like a stray.

124 ©2000 by Evan-Moor Corp. • Reading Practice at Home • EMC 4511

Page 125

What Did It Say?

Think about what you read. Choose the best answer for each question. Look at the story again if you need to.

1. Why do most people know George Washington?
   - ○ He was a brave soldier.
   - ● He was the first U.S. president.
   - ○ He was a good farmer.

George Washington's barn today

2. Where was George Washington's farm?
   - ○ Washington, D.C.
   - ○ New York
   - ● Virginia

3. How do you know farming was important to Mr. Washington?
   - ○ He liked to eat bread.
   - ● He wanted to learn the best way to farm.
   - ○ He fought in a war.

4. Why did Mr. Washington's barn make harvesting wheat easier?
   - ○ It had a ramp so the workers didn't have to go up steps.
   - ● The mules did most of the work.
   - ○ The workers didn't have to worry about rain.

©2000 by Evan-Moor Corp. • Reading Practice at Home • EMC 4511 127

Page 126

What Does It Mean?

Read the information below. Use what you learn to fill in the blanks.

George Washington used five different kinds of fences on his farms.

- The **split rail fence** was a moveable fence. It could be laid in a zigzag pattern around trees.
- The **post and rail fence** was a permanent fence. It was used to make boundary lines.
- The **hurdle fence** was a small moveable fence. It was used to keep animals in an area for grazing.
- The **waddle fence** was a tightly woven split rail fence. It was used to pen birds and small animals.
- The **living hedge** was a growing fence. It was used between fields and pastures.

A split rail fence

Write the name of the fence that would be best.

1. A fence between your property and your neighbor's property — post and rail
2. A fence around the chicken yard — waddle
3. A fence along a border with rocks and trees — split rail
4. A fence to keep the sheep in one area of the pasture — hurdle

128 ©2000 by Evan-Moor Corp. • Reading Practice at Home • EMC 4511

Page 127

Reading a Map

George Washington's big farm was called a plantation. This is a map of his plantation.

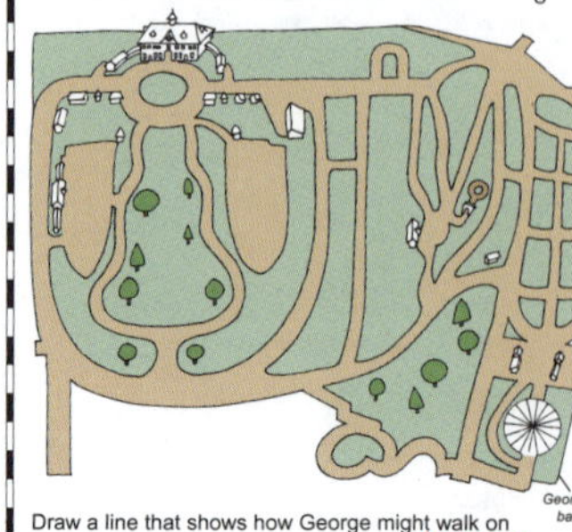

Draw a line that shows how George might walk on pathways from his house to his barn. Answers will vary.

In which direction would he have to go? southeast

©2000 by Evan-Moor Corp. • Reading Practice at Home • EMC 4511 129

Page 128

The Sounds of ea

The letters **ea** can stand for different sounds. Read the words and listen for two different **ea** sounds.

I am ready to plant the seeds.

Please take your seat.

She fixed the button with a needle and thread.

Put the hat on your head.

Mrs. White gave each of us a treat.

The words that are underlined have the **ea** sound you hear in **bread** or in **wheat**. Write each word in the column where it belongs.

bread	wheat
ready	Please
thread	seat
head	each
	treat

130 ©2000 by Evan-Moor Corp. • Reading Practice at Home • EMC 4511

Page 129

Put the Steps in Order

Cut and paste.

- Plant the wheat seeds.
- Water the seeds.
- Cut the wheat stalks.
- Take the kernels off the stalk.
- Grind the kernels into flour.
- Make some bread.

©2000 by Evan-Moor Corp. • Reading Practice at Home • EMC 4511

Page 130

Working with Word Families

alk

w + alk = w a l k   st + alk = s t a l k

t + alk = t a l k   ch + alk = c h a l k

Draw something you would see on a **walk** by a lake.

Drawings will vary.

Draw a place where you cannot **talk**.

132 ©2000 by Evan-Moor Corp. • Reading Practice at Home • EMC 4511

Page 131

Puzzle Page

Cut out the puzzle pieces. Put them together.

What do you have? George Washington's Barn

©2000 by Evan-Moor Corp. • Reading Practice at Home • EMC 4511

Page 132

Match the Opposites

Draw a line to match each pair of opposites.

plant	down
hard	slow
fast	harvest
up	less
more	easy

(plant – harvest, hard – easy, fast – slow, up – down, more – less)

Draw something that is fast. | Draw something that is slow.

Drawings will vary.

134 ©2000 by Evan-Moor Corp. • Reading Practice at Home • EMC 4511